Sacred Masque
Ensemble Rituals for Pagan Groups

Raven Kaldera

Sacred Masque

Ensemble Rituals for Pagan Groups

Raven Kaldera

Hubbardston, Massachusetts

Asphodel Press
12 Simond Hill Road
Hubbardston, MA 01452

Sacred Masque: Ensemble Rituals for Pagan Groups
© 2011 by Raven Kaldera
ISBN 978-0-9825798-8-6

All rights reserved. Unless otherwise specified,
no part of this book may be reproduced in any form
or by any means without the permission of the author.

Printed in cooperation with
Lulu Enterprises, Inc.
860 Aviation Parkway, Suite 300
Morrisville, NC 27560

*To all the good folk
in the First Kingdom Church of Asphodel,
the most welcoming religious community
I have ever known.*

Contents

Foreword: The Magic of Ensemble Rituals... i

Beltane Rites

    Beltane Rituals: The Big Circle.. 1
    Asphodel Mummer Quarter Calling 5
    Elemental Spirits Quarter Calling 6
    Seasonal Quarter Calling 8
    Dragon Beltane Rite.. 10
    Astrological Beltane.. 12
    Tarot Beltane 19
    Beltane of the Winds.. 25
    Animal Spirit Beltane 31
    Tree Spirit Beltane 35

Summer Rituals

    Summertime Rites: Sun Through Harvest 47
    Astrological Rites 49
    Multicultural Solstice 64
    Astrological Solstice Rite... 69
    Romanized Harvest Ritual.. 76
    Astrological Mabon Ritual 80

Samhain Rituals

    Samhain Rites: The Wide Game..................................... 91
    Egyptian Samhain.. 94
    Samhain in Hades.. 109
    Samhain in the Summerlands....................................... 116
    Tuonela Rite for Samhain 120
    Samhain in Helheim.. 128
    Samhain in Tibet 142
    Samhain for the Forgotten Dead 156

Yule Rituals

    Gift-Giver's Yule.. 160
    Little Red Man Folkloric Yule 167
    Hunting Of The Wren Yule Ritual............................... 170

    Astrological Winter Solstice Rite 177

Rites of Winter and Spring
    Brigid Candlemas Ritual..185
    Day of the Young Gods 190
    Astrological Ostara Rite...197

Appendix: Yule Scrolls for the Gift-Giver's Yule.............................201

Foreword: The Magic of Ensemble Rituals

When I first began looking at collections of Neo-Pagan rituals in books, it did not escape my notice that they were almost all small, intimate rites that could be performed by one or two people who knew what they were doing. It made sense – didn't the Neo-Pagan religious movement begin with traditional British Wicca, an initiatory mystery religion that began with small covens meeting in secret, often in people's living rooms or basements, with no more than thirteen members? I'd started out in a group like that myself, and for the first eight years of my Pagan life I never saw anything larger.

Until I went to a Pagan gathering for the first time, that is. Then I experienced a large group Pagan ritual with over a hundred people – five of them in a week, actually. However, even these were generally run by one or two people – usually a high priest and high priestess, in the Wiccan model – who either spoke or recited parts to the crowd, or in some cases found ways for the crowd to participate.

In following years, I went to rituals where everyone was expected to participate in some way (besides just joining hands and dancing in a circle, or intoning a group chant), and this had both positive and negative outcomes. Sometimes it created a great energetic vortex of feeling that left everyone breathless afterwards. Sometimes it created a split between the enthusiastic and the awkward and uncomfortable, the latter of which might grimly trudge through the ritual and never come back, or even flee in the middle when it became apparent that they were expected to act in ways that felt like public humiliation.

Meanwhile, the groups I was personally involved with became larger and larger. I remember how great it was when we actually got twenty people to come to our Beltane – it felt huge to have that many in my back field. These days, twenty is a small and intimate turnout, and we've occasionally topped a hundred. Even for thirty or more, one has to rethink how ritual is done. The old Wiccan model that worked well in a living room for thirteen or less no longer works when one is faced with large crowds. I remember one particularly painful Samhain ritual enacted by a well-known Wiccan group that was well-advertised enough to draw 400 people from several states. They adapted their ordinary rite, which included lots of droning on and on by the high priest and high priestess, and purifications for all the "inner circle" ... but not the 400 people standing around shivering and watching a coven, in essence, have its rite in front of them. At one point, when they took "cakes and wine" in front of all the shivering people, practically ignoring them, it hit home to me how badly Neo-Paganism needed to break out of the traditional Wiccan ritual format. That structure just doesn't work when you've got twenty-five people, much less fifty or a hundred.

Traditionally, when the British Wiccan coven got large enough it was supposed to "hive off", but many people today are asking for something that is more akin to a church with a congregation, where they show up for services with a whole community of people, are given a spiritual experience of some sort, have refreshments, and go home. Unlike the mystery tradition model where teaching about the faith is done in separate sessions, modern congregational Pagan rituals often have a certain amount of education – subtle or blatant – as part of the rite itself, because showing up for high holidays may be the only religious involvement that many people will have with the group.

Some Pagans decry this trend, saying that Paganism should not go down the road of church-on-Sunday Christianity, and that the whole point of Paganism is a whole-life experience, which is not untrue. However, to insist on a mystery-tradition framework for all Pagans excludes a great number of people whose lives are just too busy to commit to this, especially as there are still far fewer Pagan groups than there are, say, Christian churches, and Pagans may have to travel pretty far to find the group whose doctrine and fellowship works for them. There needs to be a place for congregational Pagans in our demographic, because they exist – actually, the hard truth is that there are probably far more would-be congregational Pagans than there are Pagans who will ever muster the dedication and time commitment that an initiatory mystery religion requires.

When we began the First Kingdom Church of Asphodel in 1999, it grew out of an eclectic Pagan living-room group that kept getting more members and realized that it needed a different kind of structure. We adopted a congregational model, and have never regretted it. This model does mean that our membership differs from that of smaller, more intimate groups. For one thing, we never kick anyone out unless their behavior at events is bad enough to be a serious problem to others. We don't kick them out because they are awkward or dorky or mildly autistic-spectrum, or will never be anyone's friend, or are slightly mentally ill (but not enough that they can't control their behavior) or have Tourette syndrome and occasionally bark during ritual, or are physically disabled, or are covered in tattoos or piercings, or whose gender cannot be determined by their appearance. Smaller groups, to maintain their intimacy, have to screen more heavily. That's why congregational groups so often get the people who cannot find small, intimate groups to join, as well as people who could perhaps be accepted in one but simply don't have the time to spend, and want to be able to come to the occasional high holiday and nothing more.

Because of this, we've had to create rituals that have varying levels of participation, from staff to silent bystander. It's important to us to make comfortable both the diva who wants to dress up in a costume and read a part every single time, and the hermit who would prefer to stand in the back and do nothing but watch every time. Theatrical ensemble rituals work well for this, because there are a number of (often adjustable) parts for divas, and usually some minimally participatory parts for everyone else, and if there are a few hanging back and not joining in at all, the drama of the ritual will still give them some measure of spiritual experience without making them uncomfortable.

In addition, "performance-style" rituals can be highly educational. If nothing else, they can subtly teach about a particular worldview. They can, in essence, be small mystery plays. Some of them, of course, are outright large mystery plays. They entertain and by doing so, they sink lessons into people's heads. Whether we like it or not, much of the reason that traditional austere Christian churches are losing people to charismatic sects is because the latter take their religious entertainment very seriously. While the more "dignified" churches – and many Neo-Pagans – look at the idea of prioritizing religious entertainment as pandering or selling out, it must be acknowledged that it is a fair way to get a message across.

I define an ensemble ritual, for purposes of this book, as *a rite requiring five or more people, including the main officiant, enacting some kind of symbolic or folkloric performance that probably requires at least a perfunctory rehearsal beforehand, for a larger audience of people who will watch and participate only peripherally when instructed.* It is certainly not the only ritual style that works for large groups, but it is definitely useful for that situation. As long as the ensemble cast manages to get in some practice and figure out what they are doing, it can work for a walk-in group of total strangers, some of whom may still not be sure what "all this Pagan stuff" is really about. They can walk in, feel no pressure, and walk out again with more knowledge than they arrived with.

These rituals were all written for the First Kingdom Church of Asphodel over a period of a decade and a half, and have all been tested on one of the most varied yet incredibly welcoming Pagan groups I've ever had the privilege to be in. Our hard work is your gift. Take these rites and adapt them as you will to your own group's sacred days.

RAVEN KALDERA
MAY 2010

Beltane Rites

Beltane Rituals: The Big Circle

Beltane is the biggest event in our church year. Instead of a one-afternoon ritual, we long ago expanded it to a whole weekend. People come in and set up their tents on Friday night so that they can roll out of their bedrolls on Saturday morning and be ready for the Maypole ritual. The first part always goes the same way: The couple chosen to be the Green Man and May Queen come to the front area of the property where the farm lies, and ritually water our orchard and feed some hay to our animals. This ensures a fertile year for our fruit and livestock – and yes, we really do believe that it works – and also reminds everyone of out links to the old agricultural ways of our ancestors. The ritual staff gets their costumes (often with their lines on index cards pinned discreetly to the inside of mummer wings or the back of pole banners), does a last-minute line check, and then the staff and the Sacred Couple process to the back woods and field, where the campers are sleepily eating their breakfast (even though it is almost noon).

Unlike other ritual staff parts, choosing a Green Man and a May Queen is more than just picking two random people. This ritual needs a couple who can embody and channel the energy of the fertility of the Earth. While our Pagan church is dedicated to equal gender opportunity, and any other part in any other ritual can be performed by any physical body as far as we are concerned, the Green Man and May Queen need to be one male-identified, physically fertile male, and one female-identified, physically fertile female. They can be using any sort of birth control, but cannot be sterilized. They should ideally be in some sort of personal relationship, one serious enough that they aren't going to break up four days before the ritual and leave us scrambling to find replacements.

The folk are divided into three groups for the ritual in our church – the men, the women, and those who identify as both and/or neither. The third gender people (well, the early risers among them, at least) have already been in the woods before most people arose, and hidden the Maypole somewhere in the forest surrounding the ritual field. We've learned to be careful about where we hide it – it can't be too hard to find or everyone will be standing around, but conversely, it can't be so easy that they're back in no time. The men are dispersed to find it, led by the Green Man. Meanwhile, the May Queen and the rest of the women clear out the stone-filled hole that lies in the center of our great circular labyrinth, where the Maypole stands from Beltane to Samhain. They pour in offerings of fresh raw milk, eggs from our farm, beer or wine or mead, a few coins, and some bread. The third gender group decorates the Maypole wreath with flowers, tiny wind chimes, and other small shiny items.

When the men return with the Maypole, they carry it three times around the field while chanting – we've tried to come up with various original chants but every year they all seem to revert to the old "Pan, Woden, Baphomet, Cernunnos, Osiris" – and then pause at the entrance to the labyrinth. Here the third gender group attaches the wreath and the ribbons to the pole, and then forms a human chain between the men with the pole and the women circling the hole, slowly bringing them together. We've found that it's important to check that the pole is sturdily embedded; our current head of event security (who happens to be a man) always checks it quietly, and tells the men if it needs more stones or to be tilted in any particular direction. We've found that it's good to detail someone for this job, especially since ours has to be an erection that will last for six months.

When the pole goes upright into the hole, there is always a moment of Something – a kind of charge from Earth to Sky, as if we'd actually plugged it into a socket. Even people who have never experienced a Pagan ritual look big-eyed and wide-mouthed, and later say, "That was ... something! I don't know what, but it was ... something!" (Yes. It was the energy created by doing the same ancient archetypal ritual in the same place for year after year after year.)

Then the Green Man and May Queen come forward and do their bit around the pole – one chases the other and finally catches and kisses them. We let each year's couple decide who is going to chase whom – sometimes it's the Green Man, sometimes the May Queen. Then the Maypole is danced while our church choir sings Beltane songs, including the millennium-old *Sumer Is Icumen In*. Others might include Jethro Tull's *Cup Of Wonder*, Annwfn's *Bringing In The May*, Loreena McKennitt's *Mummer's Dance*, and Gaia Consort's *Beltane Fires*.

Since newcomers may not know how exactly to dance a Maypole, we designate one person (usually a loud-mouthed person in fancy dress for visibility) to line everyone up holding their ribbons and facing each other in pairs, and telling each person whether they are starting with an "over" or an "under". Then, when the music starts, that individual calls out, "Over! Under! Over! Under!" for the first half-minute, just to make sure that everyone is getting it right. (Your group may or may not need this level of instruction.)

When the pole is done, it's time for the main ritual. This happens in the center of a large circle of people under the open sky. Everyone watching has to be able to hear and understand, and we usually encourage each speaker to talk very loud, and walk around the pole while talking, so as to make everyone feel included. The ritual itself can't take more than 45 minutes – everyone is standing around, they've already been standing around for some time, and they're going to get tired of it soon and want to go back to the firepit. The ritual will end with our yearly calling out of the things we are grateful for, each shout ending in "Blessings and praise!" which is echoed back to the speaker – this is expected – and then there are the yearly oaths taken on the Maypole. The main ritual has to fit between the Maypole and the shouts of praise.

It also has to be a good fit with the atmosphere of Beltane. The Maypole ritual is a showy, colorful traditional rite with lots of sentimental and archetypal value; it sets a tone of gaiety and color that must be continued, or all the energy falls too soon and people feel vaguely disappointed. One of the ways we've continued this theatrical tone is to have the four elements called by mummers in huge-winged outfits, reflecting the elements. Mummer capes are easily made out of fabric, and fringing the fabric into fluttery strips is traditional and very effective. The extended "wing" sleeves are made with three-foot sticks held in the hands; they are graceful and dance well no matter how awkward the mummer is. We usually add a matching long apron-loincloth (worn over their ordinary clothing or their skin as they choose) and a decorated half-mask for each one.

The East mummer is colored with silver-grey in the back and pastel and iridescent sunrise colors in the front, and has the most rippling fringe. Their mask is a bird mask, for Air. (Old Asphodelians will never forget the Beltane when the East mummer called the spirits of Air and an eagle immediately flew across the ritual field, crying out.) The South mummer is flame-colored with sequins and a dragon mask; the West mummer is sea-colored with white ruffles like foam and a shell-like mask. The North mummer's wings are brown and textured like bark, with many hanging strips of artificial pine garland (easily acquired at Yule) and a leafy mask. People either wear appropriately-colored clothing under the cape or, in some cases, go naked save for the cape, mask, and apron.

Mummer costumes also go well with giant full-head masks, because both the mask and the wings can be fastened to a shoulder harness, which will keep the weight of the large mask (usually of papier-mâché) off the head of the mummer. Giant heads can also be worn with stilts – for safety's sake large-footed wide stilts under a long skirt are best – and the mummer's "wings" can become hands and arms. Shoulder harnesses can also hold ridiculously tall headdresses, such as sun-rays or artificial trees.

Mummers make people happy. They are joyful to look at and joyful to enact. (It's also easy to pin their ritual lines to parts of their voluminous costumes.) They can be played by any gender, which is always useful for a mixed group with multiple genders.

Asphodel Mummer Quarter Calling

East Mummer:

>Hail to the Spirits of Air,
>In the name of the sword of steel!
>In the name of the shining blade!
>In the name of the whistling winds!
>In the name of the mind's edge!
>Hail and welcome!

South Mummer:

>Hail to the Spirits of Fire,
>In the name of the Wand of Light!
>In the name of the flaming torch!
>In the name of the summer tree!
>In the name of Will and Power!
>Hail and welcome!

West Mummer:

>Hail to the Spirits of Water,
>In the name of the cup of wine,
>In the name of the beating heart,
>In the name of the ocean's tides,
>In the name of the rivers of blood.
>Hail and welcome!

North Mummer:

>Hail to the Spirits of Earth,
>In the name of the five-pointed star!
>In the name of the five senses!
>In the name of the body's limbs!
>In the name of the apple's heart!
>Hail and welcome!

Elemental Spirits Quarter Calling

East Mummer:

>Spirits of the East, Powers of Air!
>Laughing sylphs that ride the winds,
>Faery dancers laughing on the breeze,
>Pixies in the morning's meadow,
>Sprites that fly on gossamer wings!
>Devas of the Realms of Air,
>Be with us!
>We come before you with open eyes,
>Glorying in the rising sun of spring!
>Let this day be a new beginning for all of us!

South Mummer:

>Spirits of the South, Powers of Fire!
>Flaming phoenix of rebirth,
>Salamander walking unharmed through flames,
>Dragon sleeping on riches and breathing fire,
>Faery horses striking sparks from your hooves!
>Devas of the Realms of Fire,
>Be with us!
>We come before you with open spirits,
>Glorying in our freedom from the winter!
>Let this day create our future anew!

West Mummer:

>Spirits of the West, Powers of Water!
>Naiads of the flowing rivers,
>Undines of the oceans deep,
>Mermaids singing siren's songs,
>Tritons swimming with the dolphins!
>Devas of the Realms of Water,
>Be with us!
>We come before you with open hearts,
>Glorying in the circle of community that heals us!
>Let this day teach us that we are never alone!

North Mummer:
>Spirits of the North, Powers of Earth!
>Dryads who safeguard the great trees,
>Gnomes who mine the depths underground,
>Elves of the forests walking silent trails,
>Deep faeries of the hidden caves!
>Devas of the Realms of Earth,
>Be with us!
>We come before you to be at home in our bodies
>And glory in the solid truth of our flesh!
>Let this day teach us that we are Earth,
>And Earth is sacred,
>And we are sacred.

After the rite is over, each element is thanked in more informal language, and everyone cries out "Hail!" after each of the four quarters. For us, this usually happens after the last person who wishes to make an oath on the pole has finished, which gives closure to the ritual.

Seasonal Quarter Calling

East Mummer:

    Spirits of the Winds, we call you!
    Hail and welcome on this day of Spring
    When your brisk winds
    Bring the scent of green leaves
    Just opening from their winter sleep.
    Clear our minds of the winter slowness!
    May we wake with a deep breath
    Of the sweet-smelling year.

South Mummer:

    Spirits of the Fire, we call you!
    Hail and welcome on this day of the waxing Sun!
    We have seen the moment of equal day and night,
    And our faces are turned toward the day
    Of Summer's longest reign!
    Warm our bones, Spring's sun!
    We honor you with the great bonfire
    That sends its yearly signal to the eternal sky.

West Mummer:

    Spirits of the many Waters, we call you!
    Hail and welcome on this day of Spring,
    Season of the rain and the storm!
    The waters are thawed of their icy stillness
    And the rivers run free and wild once again.
    We pour you libation of our joy
    And celebrate the blood pounding through our veins!
    From ocean's depths to peaceful lake,
    Wash us clean with the spring rains!

North Mummer:

> Spirits of the green Earth, we call you!
> Hail and welcome on this day of your springing forth!
> The Green Man leaps for the sky,
> Gleeful with the joy of new life,
> And greets his breathless bride on this morning.
> May the Earth ring with their loving!
> May the ground shake with our footsteps
> As we dance in the paths of the Old Road tonight!

Dragon Beltane Rite

This is a very short rite, for the times when you know that your audience wants a lot of color in only a few minutes. It requires eight mummers – the four elemental mummers already described for the quarter callings, plus four more mummers play dragons. (For this rite, our South Mummer wears a flaming mask and gives their dragon mask to the South Dragon.) Their capes are wide mummer dragon wings, with thin sticks sewn into casings like the ribs of batwings. They have long stuffed tails and, of course, masks. Our Air Dragon is white, our Fire Dragon is red, our Water Dragon is blue, and our Earth Dragon is green.

Air Dragon (carrying a sword):
Now ice and snow have faded away,
And we greet the oncoming summer.
Yet we must remember
Even as we lift our arms to the sky
That the future is always uncertain.
So let this moment stand in our minds
As one perfect memory to be cherished.

Air Dragon plunges the sword into the earth.

Fire Dragon:
Hear me, O people gathered here today!
Your ancestors burned in fires
Because they would not forswear us!
Your ancestors hid in the dark
And worshiped us in secret.
Your ancestors turned to other faiths
To save themselves and their children
And forgot us, but we never left them!
Will you take up what they lay down?
Will you bring into the open what they hid?
Will you celebrate what they died for?

Fire dragon waits until all shout "We will!" then lays hands on the Maypole and blesses it.

Water Dragon:
>We water you with joy.
>We water you with the tears
>We nourish you with the hope
>Of more than three thousand years.
>May we all remember
>The fountain of ancient wisdom,
>May we all come to drink at its waters.

Water dragon pours libation at base of Maypole.

Earth Dragon *(holding a floral wreath on one wing tip)*:
>Earth, awaken to your consort,
>The sky that gives you Sun and Rain,
>The sky that calls you to reach forward
>With every tree and herb and blade of grass!
>Though summer may turn into autumn
>And yet further into winter,
>We know that the circle is eternal
>And all darkness yields again to light.
>Though these flowers may yet wither,
>What we worship lasts forever.

Earth Dragon places wreath at base of Maypole. Dragons make a circle around the Maypole, wing tip to wing tip, and dance around it.

Officiant *(during the dragon's dance)*:
>Hail to the wise ones of fire and wind,
>Of earth and water, of time and season!
>Hail to them, and may we find
>Their wisdom inside each of us!

All cry out "Hail!" At this point one could add more ritual activities, or one could call in the elemental mummers to thank the elements and close the circle.

Astrological Beltane

This ritual requires ten people to play the astrological planets; it is especially appropriate to have elemental mummers because astrology depends heavily on the four elements. Like all the rituals in this section, it ends rather abruptly. Each ritual planner should decide how these should end – an invocation by an officiant? A different ritual activity entirely? These are pieces for you to play with; use your imagination.

The planets can be mummers or just costumed people. Be creative with costumes. The Sun should wear solar colors like yellow and orange; the Moon should wear lunar colors like silver and grey. Our Mercury once wore a jacket and hat with stuffed wings pinned to it. Venus should wear rose and deep pastels; Mars should wear red and carry a spear. Jupiter wears purple and gold; Saturn wears severe black – perhaps a suit. Uranus wears neon colors and a bizarre outfit. Neptune wears flowing sea-colors and our Pluto always wears black leather and studs.

൦ൠ   ൦ൠ   ൠ൦   ൠ൦

To start the ritual, the Sun comes forward.

Sun:
> Hail all on this joyous day!
> I call upon the power of the bright Sun,
> Lord of Reason, Lord of Joy,
> Lord of the Open Eyes!
> By the power of every new day,
> I challenge all of you!
> I challenge you to see one another
> Not as you would have each other be,
> But as each of you truly are!
> Are your eyes closed to me?
> Those who would have their eyes open
> To the light of dawn,
> Come forth and receive my blessing!

Those who want the Sun's blessing come forward, and the Sun touches them on the top of their heads and says, "Welcome into the light. Go forth in happiness." Then the Moon comes forward.

Moon:
>Hail to all on this day of the Willow Tree Month!
>I call upon the power of the changing Moon,
>Lady of Mystery, Lady of Feeling,
>Lady of the Tides that wash over you all.
>By the power of your flesh and blood,
>I challenge all of you!
>I challenge you to honor that within you
>That is not reasonable, that is not rational,
>That has been with you from your birth,
>And through all your childhood,
>And will be with you when you go forth to Death.
>If what you need is to love that part of yourself,
>Come forth and receive my blessing!

Those who want the Moon's blessing come forward, and the Moon touches them on their foreheads and says, "May the Mother's love be with you. Go forth in secret knowing." Then Mercury comes forward.

Mercury:
>Hail to all travellers on this path!
>I call upon the power of Mercury,
>Spirit of flight, spirit of words,
>Spirit of the road beneath our feet
>And the path before our eyes!
>By the power of all that speaks and moves,
>I challenge all of you!
>I challenge you to shake off the winter's sloth
>And make your heels light!
>Are your feet lacking in nimbleness?
>Is your tongue slow and slacking?
>Then come forth and receive my blessing!

Those who want Mercury's blessing come forward, and Mercury flips some glitter onto them, and says, "May nothing break your stride! Go forth in swiftness!" Then Venus comes forward.

Venus:
>Hail to all on this day of beauty,
>The day when the May Queen and the Green Man
>Flaunt their courtship for all to see!
>I call upon the power of Venus,
>Lady of Love and Beauty,
>Spark of delight that resides in your heart,
>Dancer of the flesh,
>Harper of the body's music!
>By the power of Love itself,
>I challenge all of you!
>I challenge you to open yourselves to Love,
>In all its forms, pleasing and dangerous,
>Familiar and strange,
>And never to deny the stirrings of your hearts!
>Do you need more love in your lives?
>Then come forth and receive my blessing!

Those who want Venus's blessing come forward, and Venus shall kiss her fingers and touch them with perfume, or give them a kiss, as she chooses, for Love is fickle, and say, "May your heart be opened. Go forth in adoration!" Then Mars comes forward.

Mars:
>Hail to all on this day of glory!
>I call upon the power of Mars,
>Warrior and dancer in the fire,
>Defender of walls and boundaries,
>Protector of all that cannot fight alone!
>By the power of all that is driven,
>I challenge you all!
>I challenge you to fight for what you believe in
>Without thought for what pain it will give,

Or how far you might fall!
Do you lack courage in your life?
Then step forward and receive my blessing!

Those who want the blessing of Mars shall come forward, and grasp the spear of Mars, and he shall say, "Go forth in courage!" Then Jupiter comes forth.

Jupiter:
Hail to all on this day of bounty,
When the Earth begins to bring forth
What will be her gift to us all,
In the time of autumn.
Let us give thanks for her gifts,
And for all the gifts we have yet to receive!
I call upon the power of Jupiter,
Giver of gifts, Keeper of Luck,
Lord of Abundance whose hands are open to all!
By the power of all good fortune,
I challenge all of you!
I challenge you to give unto others
Even when they do not deserve it,
Even when you will get nothing from them,
And to trust that the Universe will reward you in turn!
Would you have the luck of the Universe?
Then come forward and receive my blessing!

Those who want Jupiter's blessing shall come forward, and Jupiter shall give them a coin out of his bag, and say, "Blessings upon you! Go forth in opportunity." Then Saturn comes forth.

Saturn:
Hail to all on this day
When we mark the Wheel of the Year!
I call upon the power of Saturn,
Keeper of Limits, Giver of Discipline,
Wise one of the old bones

Whose lesson is Necessity!
By the power of all endings,
I challenge all of you!
I challenge you to accept those things you cannot change,
And to discipline yourself in the face of disarray.
Is your life a mess?
Are you ready to clean it up?
Then come forth and receive my blessing,
And carry the line of your limits with you!

Those who want Saturn's blessing shall come forward, and Saturn shall make a mark upon the back of their necks with a black marker, and say, "This will give you spine! Go forth in eternity." Then Uranus comes forward.

Uranus:
Hail to all on this day of change,
For all days are days of change,
But especially ones where we come together
To see change in each other's eyes!
I call upon the power of Uranus,
Whirlwind of chaos that clears the air,
Keeper of Invention, Giver of Inspiration!
By the power of the far future,
I challenge you all!
I challenge you to tear down the limits
That you have erected for yourselves
That prevent you from reaching the horizon!
Are you bounded around by boredom?
Does dullness hound your days?
Then come forward and receive my blessing,
Which is never comfortable,
But is also never boring!

Those who want the blessing of Uranus shall come forward, and Uranus shall slap them with a strange toy, and say, "Go forth in laughter!" Then Neptune comes forward.

Neptune:

>Hail to all on this day of magic!
>I call upon the power of Neptune,
>Veiled one whose face is never seen,
>Mystical depths of the inner ocean,
>Whirlpool of madness who touches the Gods!
>By the power of all that dreams,
>I challenge you all!
>I challenge especially those who have knelt
>Before the altar of Madness
>And its blessings and pains!
>I am both the Keeper of Madness
>And the Gateway to the Gods!
>To free yourselves from the one,
>You must touch the Other!
>Will you come forth to receive my blessing,
>And find yourselves on this unseen path?

Those who want Neptune's blessing shall come forward, and Neptune shall blow bubbles at them, and say nothing. Then Pluto comes forth.

Pluto:

>Hail to all on this day,
>Which will yield to this night,
>As all days fall to night.
>I call upon the power of Pluto,
>Lord of the Funeral Pyre, Lady of the Grave,
>Who walks without fear in the darkness!
>Keeper of the fears that move in shadow
>And the fire that burns away those fears!
>By the power of all that transforms,
>I challenge all of you!
>I challenge those of you who would transform your lives
>To come forward and take from me that transformation!
>Are you desperate?
>Then this is your moment. Come to me!

Those who want Pluto's blessing shall come forth, and Pluto shall sprinkle them with ashes, and say, "Go willingly into the darkness, and go forth in regeneration."

Tarot Beltane

This ritual doesn't use all the Tarot Trumps, only the obviously personified ones. However, one could add more if one wanted. We did this Maypole ritual as part of a larger Tarot theme for the weekend. We printed up small Rider-Waite Tarot cards in several different solid colors of cardstock, one color for each card. The Trump figures in the ritual gave out one card apiece to everyone who chose to come up, but other cards were given out as well. People who volunteered for fire-tending shifts got an Ace of Wands; those who gathered firewood got a Ten of Wands. Water-carriers got an Ace of Cups for their first trip and succeeding numbers of Cups for further trips. Kitchen volunteers for the potluck feast got the Ten of Pentacles. Those who helped with parking cars or shuttling people got the Chariot. Errand-runners to the store got the Two of Wands when they left, and the Three of Wands upon returning successfully with all items. Security people got the Six of Wands. People staying for cleanup got the World card. The various activities – workshops, smaller rites, etc. – got their own minor Arcana cards related to their activities. Everyone got a Four of Wands at registration because it has maypoles on it. People were encouraged to collect as many as possible, and this definitely helped them want to volunteer for work shifts and take part in activities.

The people playing the Trumps all created their own costumes, some of them fairly elaborate. This should be encouraged with any ensemble ritual, but there should also be someone crafty who can pick up the slack for any staff members who cannot handle making a costume. Also, all costumes need to be finished and approved before the final rehearsal, with time to make a new one if one is obviously wrong, or not going to get finished.

I'd like to put a note in at this point about handing things out in ritual. While this can be a wonderful thing – giving people something to take home as a memory, a tangible marker of the ritual – it can also be awkward when there are a lot of people involved. First, we've found that people don't just walk up and grab something – most pause for a moment (or longer) to make it a more meaningful exchange. With more than twenty participants, a ritual like this can involve a lot of standing in line. For a patient or contemplative audience, that may not be a problem, but for a higher-energy group, people tend to lose focus. I suggest adding an "assistant" to help handle the line for groups from twenty to forty, adding an additional assistant for every twenty over that. This is especially important if participants are receiving something like a written note with a saying which the individual must mull over.

ཚ ཚ ྺ ྺ

Fool:
>I am the one who speaks for your wonder.
>I am the urge to flee the safety of home,
>The comfort of everything you already know.
>I am the head that turns when opportunity walks by,
>The indrawn breath before you leap off the cliff.
>Ask yourself:
>What holds you back from the new beginning?
>And, once asked, clear away the obstacles!
>Come forth and take my card, and let it spur you onward!
>For I am the first step on the road,
>And without me you will never begin.

The Magician:
>I am the one who speaks for your mind.
>I am the right word at the right moment,
>The skill that saves the ship about to be lost,
>The deft fingers that move swift and sure,
>The eyes that miss nothing,
>The tongue that gives both inspiration and trickery.
>Ask yourself:
>What is it that you want to do, but cannot,
>Because you lack the skills?
>And, once asked, go forth and learn them.
>Come forth and take my card, and add it to your magic!
>For I am the first voice on the road,

And without me you will not get far enough to hear the others.

The High Priestess:
>I am the one who speaks for hidden wisdom.
>Some of my wisdom may be found in the written word,
>Although as time passes it recedes once more
>Under a cloak of Mystery.
>Some may be found in the whisperings of Spirit into your ears.
>Listen closely! Seek deeply!
>Do not be satisfied with appearances.
>When you think that you have found the answers, ask the Gods:
>Is this true? Is this true for me?
>Is this the only truth, or are there others?
>For until you have understood many truths,
>You cannot fully understand One.
>Take my card, and keep it with all your secrets.

The Empress:
>I am the one who speaks for caring.
>I am the parent's love for the child,
>The urge to help the stricken friend,
>The wisdom that chooses to care for others
>And also to learn to care for one's self.
>I am the hand that reaches out when you are drowning,
>The one you called when you were weeping and lost.
>I am the heart that overflows with unconditional love
>For anyone who needs, whether they deserve it
>By the standards of someone else, or not –
>These standards mean nothing to me,
>And besides, you never know what a little caring
>Will do to redeem a worthless soul.
>Take my card, and hold it close,
>For those long nights when suffering is your friend.

The Hierophant:
>I am the one who speaks for tradition.
>I am the footsteps of those who have gone before us,

One and many, crying out to the Many Powers,
And being fortunate enough to receive
One small grain of knowledge.
I am all those who wrote down that knowledge
With shaking hands, who tried and tried
Until the veil was broken; who worked and worked
Until there was something secure, something real,
That could be passed on to others.
I am the tethers that keep us from falling,
The long memory,
The well-trodden path that gives us comfort in darkness.
Do not shun all the gifts of our ancestors,
For in doing so you deny the wisdom
That brought you here today.
Take my card, and remember
That these symbols are your inheritance.

Strength:

I am the one who speaks for the Will.
I am the mother who gets out of bed to tend the sick infant,
The father who drags himself to work each day
So that the family may survive,
The one who does what is difficult, without hesitation.
I am the one who keeps going, even in despair.
I am anger suppressed and replaced with compassion
Before it can do any damage.
I am the cruel word that did not leave your lips.
I am the boundary set cleanly
And defended with all your might.
I am the one who does what must be done,
Who can be depended upon, whose endurance does not fail.
Where does your strength lie?
Take my card, and hold it close to your heart.

Justice:
>I am the one who speaks for Justice.
>What is just is not always comfortable,
>Especially to all parties.
>What is just does not always feel fair,
>Especially when one is angry.
>What is just may seem terrible,
>Especially when seen with short sight.
>What is just may make you weep,
>Especially if you are human.
>But justice is the only secure platform
>On which to build for the far future.
>Take my card, and try to remember:
>That which you give, you receive in turn.

Temperance:
>I am Temperance, who speaks for balance.
>Treat your judgment and your appetite
>Like two guests in the same house, says the wise man.
>But is this what you do?
>Which of them is your favorite child –
>That which says Yes, or that which says No?
>Can you find equal love for them in your heart?
>Can you balance body and mind,
>Left and right, fire and water, heart and soul,
>Male and female, light and dark, fast and slow,
>And all dualities?
>Can you find that place which is a great plain
>And the edge of a knife blade?
>Take my card, and remember
>That overcompensation is never the answer.

The Hermit:
>I am the one who speaks for the inner voice.
>I am the wisdom that is within you
>Even if it once came from without

And that you cannot hear until you shut up.
I am the blessed silence that slows you down,
Opens you up,
Allows you to see the faraway light
That is where you should be heading.
Some part of you knows the right direction;
You need only learn to listen.
Take my card, all ye seekers on the Road,
Walkers on the Fool's Journey,
And remember that if what you seek
You find not within,
You shall never find it without.

Beltane of the Winds

For this ritual we chose to honor the Eight Winds, but also the various ancient cultures that formed and influenced modern Neo-Paganism. While we realize that there were certainly influences from other places as well – such as an influx of Eastern religion through the 1960s – we chose to focus on the Indo-Europeans and the cultures that descended from them (Greek, Roman, Celtic, Norse, Anglo-Saxon/Germanic), as well as Egyptian and Babylonian. That gave us eight winds. Some of the ritual staff were scholars in the culture they represented – we had a Hellenic Pagan for our Greek wind, a Kemetic for our Egyptian, a Norse Pagan for our Norse, etc. – and came up with the blessings themselves in the original ancient languages.

Each wore the costume of those peoples, as best as we could figure out (obviously, there is not much to go on for the Indo-Europeans, whose origins are still unknown, so we went with a simple tunic and an animal fur), and all carried poles with flags. The flags were pieces of fabric in colors relevant to the directions of the Winds – East/yellow, Southeast/orange, South/red, Southwest/purple, West/blue, Northwest/grey, North/white, Northeast/ivory – and were cut into deep pointed fringes that billowed nicely in the Beltane breezes. Each member of the ritual staff began by standing in their direction, circled completely around while talking, and ended facing outward toward their direction, with their back to the Maypole. (At the end, when all eight were standing in the middle of the circle around the Maypole, with all the flags flying, someone whispered, "It's like the Pagan UN!")

ॐ ॐ ॐ ॐ

East Wind (Greek):

Προseggize, Ω Eure, psuxhn ennoias kainismou t' empelaze.

Pro-sen-gis-de, o Eu-re, psu-khen en-noi-as kain-is-mou t' em-pel-a-ze.

Hail, fine Euros,

East Wind that blows the words of knowledge
To all our waiting tongues.
Give to us eloquence and learning
Of all the ancient wisdoms,
Whisper great thoughts in our ears
And encourage us to speak up
When many might hear us.

Southeast Wind (Babylonian):

Enüma elish lä nabû shamämü
Shaplish ammatum shuma lä zakrat

> *E-nu-ma e-lish lai na-bu-u sha-ma-mu*
> *shap-lish am-ma-tum shu-ma lai zak-rat*

Welcome Marduk, Spirit of the Southeast Wind,
Wind of the Desert Clay between the Two Sacred Rivers.
Spirit of War and Lightning, Lord Divider.
Teach us the power of the dividing blade,
Creating the boundaries between heaven and earth,
Between water and air, between the lines of each thought.
Guard our walls and keep us safe
That we may cut through all
That threatens to drown us.

South Wind (Egyptian):

Hy Neteru!
Nyś-i Rsy Meh, sedem-i!
Wenen-i hem Neter, iem en-i!
Marjiw Sekhmet, teper hen kebeh-ek neb.
Neb iem en khep em hotep
Neb 'h' wesir tep-ek.

> *Hiy net-a-roo*
> *Niysh-ee riss-ee meh, seh-dem-ee*
> *Weh-nehn-ee net-air, iy-em en-ee*
> *Mar-jeuw Sehkh-met (hard kh), tep-air hen keh-beh-ek neb*
> *Neb iy-em en (hard kh) khep em hoe-tep*

Neb (glottal stop) h (glottal stop) weh-seer tep-ek.

Hail Neteru!
I call to the Southern Wind, hear me!
I am your servant, come to me!
Beloved Sekhmet, we breathe and you purify us.
May we come and go in peace,
We stand strong before you.

Southwest Wind (Roman):

Afer Ventus, Africus.
Et itur ad astra.
Et itur ad astra.
Suus cuique mos. Suum cuique.
Meus mihi, suus cuique carus.
Mememto, terrigena.
Mememto, vita brevis.
Meus mihi, suus cuique carus.

Ah-fair Ven-toos, Ah-free-cus.
Et ee-tur ad as-tra.
Et ee-tur ad as-tra.
Soo-us kwee-kway mohss. Soo-um kwee-kway.
May-us mee-hee, soo-us kwee-kway cahr-oos.
Mem-em-toh, teh-ri-gay-na.
Mem-em-toh, vee-tah bray-vees.
May-us mee-hee, soo-us kwee-kway cahr-oos.

Welcome Africus, the Southwest Wind,
The bringer of storm and rain across the ocean
That lies in the center of our ancestral lands.
Teach us that while the storms may fly
Across the land like great raptors,
Leaving the crops bent and sodden in their wake,
They bring down from the sky the very things
That the earth desires.
Teach us not to curse the storm,

But to endure until it becomes
The warm summer rain.

West Wind (Anglo-Saxon):
Forthon cnysseth nu heortan gethohtas,
thaet ic hean streamas,
sealtytha gelac sylf cunnige,
monath modes lust maela gewhylce ferth to feran,
thaet ic feor heonan
eltheodigra eard gesece.

> *For-thon (hard th) k-nuss-eth noo*
> *hay-or-tan geh-though-tas,*
> *that ikh hee-an stree-ah-mahs,*
> *see-ahl-ti-tha gay-lahc sulf koo-ni-geh,*
> *mohn-ahth mohd-es loost maa-lah*
> *ge-hwil-cheh fairth toe fair-an,*
> *Thaat ikh fay-or hay-oh-nahn*
> *ehl-thay-oh-dee-grah ee-ahrd geh-say-chay.*

Welcome to the West Wind,
Which blew across the ocean
From the place where we now stand
To the place where our ancestors stood.
Teach us of the scent of adventure,
The longing for travel and the sea-road,
The long journey over water
That may lead to a new home.
Teach us of the yearning heart
And the evening star that guides us all.

Northwest Wind (Celtic):
Failte Bran, spiorad le Gaoth Anair Aduaidh,
Spiorad na cath, crionnacht, iomas, agus leigheas.

> *Fah-ihl-teh Brahn, spih-rrrad leh*
> *Geeh Ah-na-eer Ah-doo-ah-ee,*
> *Spih-rrrad nah cah, crih-nakht, ih-mas, ah-gus lay-ass.*

Welcome Raven, spirit of the North West Wind,
Spirit of battle, wisdom, intuition, and healing.
Teach us when to fight and when to make peace.
Teach us when to speak and when to listen.
Teach us to follow our inner guidance
Show us how to find healing in the wilderness of pain.

North Wind (Norse):

Á vindi scal við hǫggva,
veðri á sió róa.
Hvaðan vindr um kømr,
svá at ferr vág yfir;
æ menn hann siálfan um siá?
Vindsvalr heitir,
hann er Vetrar faþir
af hans vængiom
qveða vind koma
alla menn yfir.

> *Aa-ou veen-dee skahl vith hug-gva,*
> *veh-three aa-ou sith roh-wah.*
> *Kvath-an vender um kom-err,*
> *sva-ou at fairer va-oug ee-fear;*
> *Ay mehn hahn sya-oul-fan um sya-ou?*
> *Veendz-val-er hey-teer, hahn air vay-trahr fah-Theer*
> *Ahf hanss vayn-ghee-ohm, kveh-thah veend com-ma*
> *Aht-lah mayn ee-fear*

Welcome Kari, Spirit of the North Wind,
Bringer of blizzards, coldest of the cold,
Father of Frost, father of Icicle,
Grandfather of Snowflake and Snowdrift.
Stroke us with your cold, harsh winds
Laden with ice and the chilling of old bones.
Teach us of endurance, of survival,
Of what it takes to live through the winter
And still have something left to greet the Spring.

Northeast Wind (Indo-European):

Perkunas, putas heso! Xartas syem! Tod hestu!

Pair-ku-nos pu-tas hay-so! Ksar-tas su-yem! Toad hays-tu!

(Note: This may not be the correct pronunciation for Proto-Indo-European. Because it's a very dead language and there is great disagreement on how to pronounce it, we encourage people to find their own scholars and decide for themselves, or just do their best and know that the Gods are listening no matter how much you mangle the pronunciations.)

Welcome Perkunas, Lord of the Storm!
Your people blazed across the continent
Like a brush fire in the steppes,
Like a wind through the mountains,
Like a bull through the fields,
Like a boar through the woods.
All parted before them,
And here we honor you, Ancestral Storm Lord,
With your train full of the ghosts of long ago.

All stand facing outward around the Maypole with their flags, and all the people cry, "Hail!" Then the ritual can merge into something else.

Animal Spirit Beltane

The costuming and prop-work for this Beltane needed to be started months in advance, because we had to come up with animal masks for around thirteen people. We allowed folks to choose the animal tribes they would represent, and then helped them make masks (a few masks were already in existence, and some of the most crafty people were designated to make masks for the less crafty). Some were simple face-masks, some had full heads and bodies that trailed down the back (like Skunk, Salmon, and Frog). Some, like Butterfly, were less masks than full winged costumes.

For this ritual, we had participants portraying appropriate animals doing the quarter callings[,] instead of the elemental mummers. East can be any winged creature – bird or insect; South is usually a predator; West is any aquatic creature; North is a ground-dwelling creature. For casting quarters, we used the opening words of the four elemental Dragons from the Dragon Beltane ritual. The individual who chose Skunk offered to be the officiant, so Skunk does the most talking. This can be altered to any other animal if people prefer. Also, feel free to change the animal spirit lineup and create different ones – these were just the ones our folk wanted to portray.

If you think that it is appropriate for your group, you can put out a can for donations to an appropriate charity, such as the World Wildlife Fund, and suggest after the ritual that people might like to contribute. After all, it's all very well and good to say that we as Pagans will work toward saving the animal tribes, but we ought to be willing to actually do something besides talk. While asking for money during ritual is in poor taste, having a donation can ready afterwards, while it's still fresh in everyone's mind, can be a non-pressuring way to raise some funds toward a cause.

ೞ   ೞ   ೞ   ೞ

Skunk Mummer (Officiant):
We are the spirits of the tribes of this land!
We crawl and fly, we run and climb,

And we were here before you, all of us!
We are the guardians of this land,
Though you do not know it,
Because our fate is wound with this land,
And so is yours as well,
Although you act as if you do not know it.
We honor this land, and we make it offerings
Every year, of our flesh and blood.
You, yourselves, you must offer as well!
What will you offer to the Earth?

Deer Spirit *(laying down an antler at the Maypole)*:
> I give my speed, my glory,
> And my body to be eaten when it is necessary
> For the cycle to continue.

Coyote Spirit *(laying down an animal skull)*:
> I give my cunning, my teeth,
> And my ability to clean up the mess
> Of every dead body that lies on the earth.

Butterfly Spirit *(laying down flowers)*:
> I give beauty and joy
> And the dance of a single season,
> And the ability to need nothing more than that.

Frog Spirit *(offering a glass bowl of clear glass marbles in water)*:
> I give the fragile lives of all my children
> Who are the indicators of abuse and pollution,
> Whose lack of incarnation are Nature's protest.

Salmon Spirit *(offering a string of wooden fish)*:
> I give the excitement of the rushing river
> And the wild mating that makes us anew,
> And my flesh to be eaten when it is done.

Cat Spirit *(bringing a bit of meat)*:
> I give sleekness and silence
> And sharp eyes in the bushes,
> I give alliance with both human and the wild.

Dog Spirit *(bringing a leash)*:
> I bring ten thousand years of loyalty,
> The work of being the guardian of Mankind,
> And the hope of Mankind's love and trust in animals.

Sparrow Spirit *(laying down a streamer of ribbons)*:
> I bring the song of dawn
> And the hope of every morning,
> And the knowledge that the sky is always love.

Hawk Spirit *(laying down a claw)*:
> I bring the gift of long sight
> And seeing the big picture,
> The ability to choose and dive from the sky.

Bear Spirit *(laying down a small stuffed bear)*:
> I bring the gift of the long sleep
> And rising again from the winter
> To prepare and greet the spring.

Bee Spirit *(laying down a cup of honey)*:
> I bring the gift of industriousness
> And the never-ceasing work,
> To make nourishment out of beauty.

Snake Spirit *(laying down a long ribbon)*:
> I bring the gift of deep wisdom,
> Of the dark places in the body of Mother Earth,
> Of the path to regeneration.

Skunk Mummer (Officiant):
> Our ancestors were not all born on this land.
> Many came from across the sea,
> And took part in the great thievery

Of this land from Her people.
Yet here we are, so many of us,
Our souls born on this land,
Our bodies made of nourishment grown on this land,
Our hearts full of the beauty of this land.
We are the children born of years of rape,
Of centuries of destruction,
Yet we have the chance to make amends
By honoring and caring for
The treasure beneath our feet.
We stand here as the bridge
Between the country of our ancestors
And the country of our birth.
Will you join us in this work?

All shout "We will!"

Tree Spirit Beltane

(This ritual is derived, with permission, from the *Pagan Book of Hours* of the Order of the Horae.)

We brought in a small table and laid it with six trays, containing a jug of birch beer and many cups; a bowl of maple syrup; crackers spread with hawthorn jelly; cookies made from acorn flour; a bowl of hazelnuts; a plate of apple slices; and a bowl of water, some pine soap, and towels. Those portraying the Trees wore tabards with printed leaves of the right sort (or apples, for Apple Tree) on them, and twig wreaths.

For each round, people were invited to come up to take the offered food if they wanted that tree's blessing. Some people came up for every round, and some came up just once or twice. The initial suggestion for Maple was for people to simply dip their fingers in the bowl of maple syrup. That may not be objectionable in a small group, but many folks are not interested in sticking their fingers into food that thirty other people have just stuck their fingers in. We decided to get rolled wafer cookies to dip in the maple syrup. (Do be sure to get pure maple syrup, not maple-flavored "pancake syrup".)

Similarly, with the birch beer, we decided to have individual small paper cups, instead of all drinking from one large goblet. For Oak, we ordered a small bag of acorn flour from a specialty shop, and after two failed attempts at acorn flour crackers, we made some very tasty little cookies. For Hazel, we had hoped to get whole hazelnuts, but finding only finely chopped hazelnuts in the store, we substituted cookies covered in Nutella (a chocolate-hazelnut spread) and sprinkled with chopped hazelnuts. For Pine, the initial suggestion was pine nuts. However, in the interest of not leaving our guests with sticky fingers for the rest of the ritual, we decided on a ritualized handwashing with pine soap.

Whenever you share food in ritual, it is good to be aware of the possibility of food allergies in your participants. For instance, we might have a few gluten-free cookies or crackers set aside for one of our members. In other cases, substitution is not appropriate – if someone is allergic to hazelnuts, they'd either have to skip that part or take a cookie but not eat it. Unless there is some ritual reason not to, food shared in ritual should be portioned into "bite-sized" individual servings.

This ritual ends in a "call and response" blessing where the officiant recites a line, and the congregation repeats it back. When doing call-and-response prayers, keep in mind that the intent is to engage the audience, not challenge their powers of memorization. You may want to split the lines in this prayer if you think people will stumble over them. ("By seeds of all beginnings" "May our magic spring skyward.")

ଓଃ ଓଃ ଚ ଚ

Officiant:
>There are those who mock us for worshiping trees,
>But the trees are our oldest ancestors,
>Protecting us in their branches before we could speak,
>Giving us their bodies when we learned to build,
>Giving us their children to eat,
>Their leaves to drink,
>Their bark to ease our pain,
>And their bloodlines to twist to our will.
>This year we thank the Green Man,
>The living embodiment of all our tallest green spirits.

Birch Tree comes forward.

Officiant:
>Hail, Green Man of the Winter!
>The forest burns like a torch
>Leaving only a field of ash
>And the burned skeletons of sticks.
>We stand on the crematoriums
>Of a hundred layers
>Of a hundred fires
>Which nourish the Earth.
>And yet, every time,

It is you, Birch Tree,
Who forges ahead into the meadow,
Whose sprouts come forth from the ash
Who is the first to leap forth
From the Mother's flesh.

Birch Tree:

I am Frigga's blessing,
I am Danu's pride,
I am the stag of seven tines,
I am the pheasant who survives the winter,
I am the new green from the ashes,
I am the White Lady of the Woods
Whose touch brings healing
And sometimes madness!
Would you learn to nurture yourself,
To take care of your body and mind,
To ease your way, step by step,
Back from pain and madness?
This is the gift I give –
Come forward and receive my blessing!

People who choose to, come forth and get a sip of birch beer.

Maple Tree comes forward.

Officiant:

Hail, Green Man of the Winter and Spring!
Your secret blood rises
With the first teasing thaw,
Amid the chill winds and snow.
We drink of your blood,
And you give it willingly,
Sacrificing your life force
That we may have sweetness.
For happiness is no luxury,
It is our right and our delight.

You who bleed for our pleasure,
You who give us your innermost gift,
You who flame like a torch in the autumn
And warm our tongues in the spring,
We hail you, sacred Maple,
Green Man of the Winter and Spring,
On this the time of your rising.

Maple Tree:

I am the tree of beauty,
I am the tree of nourishment,
I am the fire of a hundred hills
Lit from the first spark of autumn.
I am the wild turkey who gives of its flesh,
I am the guardian of this land we live on,
The tree that watches over the life
Of this, our cold New England.
Do you lack sweetness in your life?
Would you have respite from sorrow?
Do you wish kindness to smile on you?
This is the gift I give –
Come forward and receive my blessing!

People come forth and dip a cookie in the maple syrup.

Hawthorn Tree comes forward.

Officiant:

Hail, Green Man of the Spring!
Hawthorn of the Day of Love
Whose great thorns stab and slice
As painfully as the bonds of Love
Do to our hearts.
That which gives the greatest joy
Must also give the greatest pain,
If only in its absence,
And this is a truth you teach us,

Highest ring on the Maypole,
Overseer of the greening games,
Watcher over the loving couples.

Hawthorn Tree:

I am beloved of the singing thrush,
I am cruel as Blodeuwedd,
I am beautiful as Hymenaeus,
I am the dance of Maia,
I am the friend of the faeries
Whose purple berries work such
Action on the heart,
I will have no exclusive pairing,
But only the rampant maddening Love
That is both curse and greatest blessing.
Is your life dull and drab?
Are you lacking in passion?
Are you looking for love? Or even more love?
This is the gift I give –
Come forward and receive my blessing!

People come forth and get hawthorn jelly on crackers.

Oak Tree comes forward.

Officiant:

Hail, Green Man of the Summer!
Great Oak Tree of grandeur,
Your roots extend as far beneath
As your branches spread above,
Living avatar of the cosmic reflection.
Oak king, you who give your life
Every year at the midsummer,
Teach us when to stand strong
And when to gracefully yield.
We hail you, sacred Oak King,
Green Man of the Summer,

On this your day of greatest triumph.

Oak Tree:
> I am the royal emblem of Zeus,
> Tree of the gods of Kings,
> Lightning's tree, struck from above,
> Exploding in wrath, dying in flames,
> Green shaft of the colossal Dagda,
> Mighty as jovial Thor,
> Staff-rune of Angrboda,
> Fuel of the midsummer fires,
> Stout guardian of the door,
> The throne of two-faced Janus.
> Are you weak and yielding in your life?
> Do you lack strength and endurance,
> The ability to stand firm and tall
> In the face of every storm?
> This is the gift I give –
> Come forward and receive my blessing!

People come forth and get acorn cookies.

Hazel Tree comes forward.

Officiant:
> Hail, Green Man of the Summer!
> Hazel tree who is teacher of art and science,
> Knowledge and beauty bound up as one,
> You show us that they should not
> Ever be separated, lest we lose
> One half of our selves.
> Arbiter, mediator, herald
> Of any side that calls you,
> You teach us to see things fairly
> From the bard's perspective
> Where Truth rules first and foremost
> And yet can be wrapped in Story.

We hail you, sacred hazel tree,
Green Man of the Summer,
With this your gift of our sustenance.

Hazel Tree:

I am the kernel of the bard's joy,
Wisdom in a nutshell,
Concentrated nourishment
Of the body and the soul.
Salmon of wisdom in Connla's spring,
Magical crane-bag of the poets,
Diviner's rod, searching out
The hidden mysteries
And sharing them with all who seek,
Would you have eloquence in your words?
Would you be accounted wise
And study easily, knowledge falling
Like ripened nuts into your hands?
This is the gift I give –
Come forward and receive my blessing!

People come forward and get hazelnuts.

Apple Tree comes forward.

Officiant:

Hail, Green Man of the Autumn!
Apple tree of immortality
Whose branches hide the white hind,
Whose fruit nourishes all,
Whose juice gives gladness
To those who work your Earth,
Whose seeds show the pentad
Of the eternal Goddess,
Equal to the lowest in their folly
And fate; this is your gift,
Love-fruit, merry one,

Brightest star in the harvest
With the universal star at your core.
Teach us that this joy
Belongs to everyone,
As does your gift of health,
So may we all be hale!
We hail you, sacred apple tree,
Green Man of the Autumn,
On this your day of greatest nourishment.

Apple Tree:

I am the blessing of Iduna's gold,
The fruit of immortality,
The bliss of Pomona of Rome,
The orchards of Helheim
And of the Summerland.
I am the tool of Eris who shows
How the mighty may fall
Beneath my spreading branches.
Is your flesh plagued with ill health?
Would you love your body?
Would you have escape from sickness?
This is the gift I give –
Come forward and receive my blessing!

People come forward and get sliced apples.

Pine Tree comes forward.

Officiant:

Hail, Green Man of the Winter!
Pine tree who keeps its needles
Throughout all the coldest months,
Haven of the forest spirits,
We bring you into our homes with joy!
Gilded king for a moment,
A day, a season, a whisper of time

And then laid down to death.
Yet your secret is rebirth
And immortality, that moment
Of translation between the two
That we will only see once
And that at the end of our days.
We hail you, sacred pine tree,
Green Man of the Winter,
On this your day of rebirth.

Pine Tree:

I am the tree of Attis, the slain youth
Cut down for a hundred purposes,
Quick to light and quick to burn
And quick to bring cheer,
I am timber of benches and puncheons,
I am the whisperer in the winter night,
I am the singer in the frost-nipped winds,
I am the Lord of the northern forests,
I am the speaker to animals,
I am the guardian of the track
Of great stag-horned Herne.
I am the oldest of all the trees,
Evergreen before their leaves were ever born.
Would you know the secret of rebirth?
Would you remain green through hard times?
Would you know the wisdom of the oldest ways?
This is the gift I give –
Come forth and receive it!

People come forth and Pine Tree gives them a purificatory handwashing with the pine soap and water.

Officiant (call and response):

By seeds of all beginnings, may our magic spring skyward.
By roots of all depths, may we stand strong in our convictions.
By stem and trunk that reaches for the sky, may our spirits soar.

By bud that grows, may our dreams never be crushed.
By leaf that kisses the Sun and rain,
May we share our joys and sorrows.
By flower that opens to the dawn,
May we learn to trust in each other and in the Gods.
By fruit that gives forth sweetness, may we nourish each other.
By seed within the fruit that grows the tree anew,
We shall live, and live again each Spring,
By life and death, by Lord and Lady,
By hand and eye, by heart and spirit,
As all green things grow, so shall our faith,
And its memory be carried forever beneath the feet
Of a thousand generations to come.

Summer Rituals

Summertime Rites: Sun Through Harvest

Our summer holidays – Solstice, Lammas, and Mabon – tend to be simpler and less theatrical, as we concentrate on such things as the yearly Solstice haul of a standing stone into our stone circle.

One of the problems we've had at hot-weather rituals is keeping people standing for hours in bright sunlight and heat, plagued by biting insects. Have some kind of shade and chairs for those with physical problems, and have a jug of water and some cups at hand somewhere discreet in the circle. It's no good as an experience if people pass out, or have to leave, or can't concentrate because they are sweating buckets and thirsty. Cleansing water poured over the head as a ceremonial purification works well in many summer rituals. Remember also that staff people have worse memories for lines and blocking after standing in the heat for too long.

This brings us to a question that many people doing theatrical rituals have: Should people be required to memorize lines, or can they read off a sheet of paper? The answer is: It depends. If they are supposed to be saying lines while doing some important activity that requires both hands, make sure that you pick someone for that part who can memorize lines. Many people can't, or rather even if they memorize them, the lines will suddenly vacate their heads as soon as they are faced with a roomful or field full of people. In general, our policy is to have lines written out for as many people as is reasonably possible. For "characters" who need only stay in one place, we've often pinned index cards with their lines to their outfits.

We have also made eight sets of four tabards and banners for the high holidays, for the callers of the quarters, in seasonally appropriate cloth. This was a matter of haunting the fabric stores for a few years and picking up printed cotton fabrics when the right seasons came along. The tabards are simple and shield-shaped; the banners are similarly shaped and hang from their cross-poles on tall poles. Each element is portrayed differently for each season – Water is white and silver ice at Yule, waterfalls at Beltane, deep sea at Solstice. Fire is a red velvet hearthfire at Yule, a fire of red roses at Beltane, and the Sun at Solstice. Earth is a snow-covered scene at

Imbolc and spring flowers at Ostara; Air is birds at Ostara, starry nights at Beltane, and winter winds at Yule. The best thing about the banners themselves, however (besides looking impressive when they proceed in), is that all sorts of invocations can be taped to the poles behind them, and no one needs to be any the wiser.

Astrological Rites

This book has already provided you with one astrological ritual (and contains several more seasonal ones), but astrological events are continually happening all the time. Some of them are fairly major, and building a ritual around them can take that energy – the energy of the cosmic clock and its synchronicity – and use it toward creating manifestation in the world. However, it's impossible to write such specific rituals in advance, considering that time marches on and the sky changes continually. You who may read this ten years or more after the publication of this book will have to create your own rites around the major astrological activity going on then. However, to that end, we'll describe one ritual that we did around an important moment in the year 2009, to inspire you to shape your own.

This was created as the main ritual of a large Pagan Solstice gathering, involving around 400 people, most of whom we had to assume would know little to nothing about astrology. This meant that we had to find ways to graphically explain our point, in the middle of a large open area with a crowd of people standing around. Unless everyone in your group is experienced with astrology – or you have the time to brief every person beforehand about the symbolism – it's useful to think about how you will communicate that information to a crowd in the moment.

We had to communicate the following information: Uranus is the planet of change, chaos, nonconformity, and technology. It rules the sign of Aquarius, which has many of the same characteristics. Neptune is the planet of dreams, illusions, madness, higher spirituality, and self-sacrifice. It rules the sign of Pisces, which shares many of those characteristics as well. Those two planets entered and re-entered each other's signs for several years, a process that we call "mutual reception", which means that they are working as a team. Several astrologers got together and talked about this situation, and the ideas that came up were "Changing the Dream; Dreaming The Change". That was the inspiration for our ritual – using Uranian energy to change the undercurrent of our lives, and then using Neptunian energy to dream that change into those lives. That summer, the two planets would not only be in mutual reception, but they would move into a semisextile aspect together – a triggering angle that would put them into a very friendly relationship. The semisextile aspect would only last for a few weeks, and the gathering was right in the middle of it. The moment was perfect to take advantage of the energy, as this would not happen again for thousands of years.

The gathering at which the ritual was performed had a policy of doing three interconnected rites – two short ones at the beginning and end, and the big one in the middle. We decided to introduce the concept of astrological ceremonies in the opening ritual, in a very simple way. (This first short piece is an easy ritual that can be used outside of any specific astrological event.)

Ten people were chosen to portray each of the planets from Sun to Pluto, and dressed in appropriate costumes. They were chosen because they embodied that planetary energy in some way. Drummers were recruited beforehand, and asked to perform ten different rhythms for about five minutes each. The description of each planet's qualities were given to each person portraying them – the Sun's bright and cheerful, Mars's aggressive and warrior-like, Saturn's disciplined and regimented, and so forth.

ଔ ଔ ଽ ଽ

To begin the ritual, the officiant stood forward and said:

Officiant: The planets and stars are part of the rhythm of life. Turning in the sky-wheel, they teach us about all the different paths of existence. Later this week, at the main ritual, you will meet two of the planets and learn their lessons. In the meantime, we present the other planets in the solar system! Dance with them! Dance in the rhythm of life!

Then each planet stood forward, spoke their opening piece, and the drumming started. People danced to the rhythms for ten minutes, with the planet-performer dancing in the middle, and then the next planet took their place. The opening lines were as follows:

Sun: I am the Sun! I am the center of all things, the essential Self! I am consciousness, warmth, joy, and life! I am the Light that dawns, and illuminates all things! Dance with me now, and know your true self!

Moon: I am the Moon! I am your night side, your emotions, all the treasure and trash left from your childhood. I am the inner child and the inner parent. I am the quiet voice of intuition, and the raging feelings that threaten to drown you. Come dance the ebb and flow of the tide with me, and know what lies within!

Mercury: I am Mercury! I think fast, I talk fast, I move fast, I am the power of thought! I am words and letters and numbers and motion – moving, moving, moving! I am the silver tongue, the golden touch, the mind like a steel trap! Dance with me now – and stay on your toes!

Venus: I am Venus! I am the force of love in all its forms, honey! I am the seeker of beauty, I am the open cup of the heart! I am the sigh you give when you see a sunrise, a waterfall, the naked body of your lover! Dance the dance of love with me!

Mars: I am Mars! I am the warrior who defends what he believes in. I am the one who knows how to fight, to act, to strike when the iron is hot! What would you fight for? Dance that passion with me now!

Jupiter: I am Jupiter! I am the Giver of Gifts and the force of luck. I am abundance – there's plenty here for everyone! I'm your favorite uncle. I'm the guy with the Good Stuff! Dance for me now!

Jupiter did not dance, but tossed fake coins to the crowd one at a time. Saturn stepped forward, and stopped the drumming dead silent with a motion.

Saturn: I am Saturn. I am the force of discipline, the one who says that you must work as well as play. I'm the principal of the school of Hard Knocks. What you get for free must be paid for. Dance now, but remember that the work will be there when you are done.

Instead of dancing, Saturn walked around the circle. When she came to someone who had one of Jupiter's coins, she held out her hand for it. If they refused to give it up, she gave them a cold glare and moves on. If they handed it over, she favored them with a nod.

Pluto: I am Pluto. I am the darkness deep within you, the darkness that is also the place of power. What can kill can cure, I say, and what does not kill me makes me stronger. Where is your hidden power? Dance your darkness now, and bring on the night!

All danced, and then the officiant said:

Officiant: Go forth into the night, but take the memory of what rides the skies with you! We will come together again in three days, and then we will see what gifts the skies have for us!

ଔ ଔ ଓ ଓ

On the day of the main ritual, we brought together a staff of nineteen people. Four represented the elements – also important astrological concepts – and called the quarters. Four more played Uranus, Neptune, Aquarius, and Pisces. Ten more people played archetypes of the two planets, six for each one. In addition, there was an officiant. We had also made a huge wheel of glued layers of cardboard, about six feet in diameter with a rim about 18" across, and an "axle" through the center so that it could be rolled about by two additional volunteers. The wheel was sprayed black and dotted with stars like the night sky, representing the star-wheel that turns eternally. We made two large circles of canvas which could be tied to anchor points on the wheel; one was plain and the other was covered in small string ties sewn onto the outside of it. These were laid aside at the beginning of the rite.

ଔ ଔ ଓ ଓ

To begin the ritual, the wheel was rolled through the ritual space naked with its painted night sky revealed.

Each of the persons representing the elements stood forward with banners decorated with appropriate symbols and called the quarters.

Air:
>Hail to the Guardians of the Air!
>Mercury who inspires our minds,
>Who gives us the words to tell our stories,
>We raise our voices in thanks!
>Uranus whose far vision sees beyond all boundaries,
>We hail your winds of change on this day!
>Hail!

Fire:
>Hail to the Guardians of the Fire!
>Sun who shines your rays down upon us,
>Center of the Universe,
>We hail you with the center of our being!
>Mars, great warrior who protects us,
>Who lends your fire to all our efforts,
>Bless these efforts here today!
>Jupiter who brings luck and opportunity,
>We ask to be blessed with your warm generosity!
>Hail!

Water:
>Hail to the Guardians of the Waters!
>Turning Moon who waxes and wanes,
>Keeper of the inner parent and inner child,
>Bless our hearts on this day!
>Lovely Venus, Morning and Evening Star,
>You who stir the passions in our blood,

May you look with glorious eyes upon us!
   Ethereal Neptune, keeper of dreams,
   Inspire our imaginations with possibility!
   Hail!

Earth:
   Hail to the Guardians of the Earth!
   Ancient Saturn, Master of Discipline,
   You who know when to wait and to refuse,
   Guide our footsteps, Grandfather!
   Distant Pluto, Keeper of Prophecy,
   Shake the very ground beneath our feet
   And awake us from our slumber!
   Hail!

After this, the Elements went to the four corners of the circle, bearing their banners. When the circle split up into groups (as described in the next section), they put down their banners and joined the group of their choice. The wheel began its roll around and around the outside of the circle. Next, the officiant stood forth.

Officiant: Welcome, all folk! This week the Powers of the Heavens have come down to Earth to aid us in our Great Works! First, let me introduce our heavenly players. Welcome to Neptune, the planet of Dreams, of Poetry, of Drugs and Drink and Madness, of Becoming One with the Divine! Neptune rules the sign of Pisces, the sign of the deep ocean, of Sacrifice, of Dissolution, of Surrender!

Neptune came forth, dressed in flowing robes of soft pastel colors. He held a long scarf that matched his robes, and holding onto the other end of it was Pisces, dressed in a simple blue robe. Neptune towed Pisces into the circle to show his rulership of the sign.

Officiant: Welcome to Uranus, the planet of Change, of Chaos, of Breaking Down Boundaries! Uranus rules the sign of Aquarius, the sign of the endless space and the river of stars, of Intellect, of Inspiration, of the Future!

Uranus came forth, dressed in crazy-looking clothing and a large, brightly-colored stiffened mohawk hairdo. She held a glittering scarf, on the end of which was Aquarius, dressed in unusual neon clothing.

Officiant: In the year 1998, Neptune passed into Aquarius, where it would remain for many years, as these planets are great and slow. *(Uranus handed over the scarf with Aquarius, and the planets moved apart – Neptune with two planets in tow – circled around one full circle, and came back to the center.)* On New Year's Day of 2004, Uranus passed into Pisces, where it too would remain for many years. *(Neptune handed over the scarf with Pisces to Uranus, and the two again moved apart, circled, and came back together.)* Astrologers call this Mutual Reception, when two planets are in each other's signs, and it signifies that they are a team, working together for the same goals. This will not happen again between these two planets for thousands of years. And this year – this summer, these bare few months – the two of them move into the same degree, in a position called semisextile, linked together in friendship.

The officiant held up yet another string, this one decorated with all sorts of interesting things, and held the two ends out to the two planets as they came together. They each took a string end and moved apart until it was held taut and stopped them. This made a human chain of all four people, with strings, chains, and scarves between them, stretching across the circle.

Officiant: So for this moment, this short time, the Cosmos has granted us the right to make change in the world through the dreams that we all dream. So it is that we come together here, Changing the Dream and Dreaming the Change. Yet we all have different dreams, and we all make change in different ways. Because of this, Uranus and Neptune wear many different faces. Which of them do you follow?

At this point, the twelve faces of Uranus and Neptune came forward. Six lined up on the side of Uranus and six on the side of Neptune. They introduced themselves one at a time. First was the Mad Scientist, dressed in a white lab coat and carrying a strange gadget that beeped and lit up and crackled with electricity.

Mad Scientist: I am the Mad Scientist! My dreams and manic, obsessive creations change the world! Join me, my glorious nerds and geeks, and we will create tomorrow's techno-magic! Join me, fellow eggheads, and if we can't blind 'em with our brilliance, we'll baffle 'em with our bulldada! Join the ranks of Da Vinci, Tesla, and Reich! Follow me and release the insane genius within!

Next was the Trickster, dressed in brightly colored harlequin clothing with a silly hat.

Trickster: I am the little child who points out that the emperor has no clothes. I make the joke that causes you to both smile and wince because it cuts so close to the bone. I identify the hard truth hidden behind a pretty mask. I reveal ugly lies dressed up in fancy clothes. I'm one who forces you to admit your folly by making you believe at first that it's someone else's folly. I am both innocence and wisdom, irreverence and seriousness. I am the Trickster, and if you would learn to laugh at what you see, and thus to laugh at yourself, come with me.

Next was the Rebel, in a leather jacket and ripped T-shirt.

Rebel: I am the Rebel. I question your traditions, your beliefs, your history, and generally everything you base your reality on. I encourage creativity, individuality, independence, and a strong sense of self. I ask questions when everyone else is happy to maintain the status quo. I shed light on new perspectives, encourage a new paradigm, and make sure the outsider is heard.

Next came Robin Hood, dressed in traditional medieval green clothing.

Robin Hood: Do you know who I am? I take care of the poor, no matter what the cost to the rich! I look after those who are the worst off. I speak for the have-nots, when the haves will not give them a voice! I am Robin Hood, and if your path in this world is to help those who society has trodden underfoot, follow me!

Next came the Sexual Pervert, dressed in tight denim shorts and a few chains and not much else.

Sexual Pervert: I am the Sexual Pervert! Do your desires run far away from Normal? Do you look at the way that the world tells you that sex should be, and say, "No! That isn't me!" Do you long for a world where your forms of loving are accepted, just one more stripe in the rainbow? If that's you, come follow me!

Next was the Healer, dressed in a long white robe.

Healer: I am the Healer. I look upon everyone with compassion, no matter who you are, no matter how ill or damaged you have become. My hands long to heal your wounds, of body, of mind, of soul. The hurt and broken flock to me, and I pour the waters of healing upon them. If your heart is that of a healer, follow me!

Next was the Artist, dressed in a handmade creative costume.

Artist: I am the Artist! I see magic with my eyes, and I make magic with my hands! The whole world is my canvas, to be painted on! There is nothing that can't be made more beautiful, or at least more interesting! If it's your path to make the world a feast for the eyes, to bring art into existence, follow me!

Next was the Madwoman, wild-haired and wild-eyed, dressed in tattered clothing.

Madwoman: I am the Madwoman! I am the soul of all who have been trapped in madness, whose mental illnesses have brought pain into their lives. I am the eyes who see the world of pain, the ears who hear the cries of dissolution. If you have lived in the Land of Crazy, if you have walked the Road of Madness, if that has shaped your path, follow me!

Next was the Monk, in a rough brown robe.

Monk: I am the Monk. I am contemplation of the divine, the path of the ascetic, the quiet way to the inner truth. I am life lived on a narrow path, without the distractions of the outside world to drown out the Spirit. I am life lived so that it gets under your skin, opens you from the inside out. If inner peace is the path you strive for, follow me!

Next was the Sacred King, dressed in hide and leaves, with antlers on his head.

Sacred King: I am the sacrificial king! I am the bean in the throat and the blood on the ground that brings the rain. I am the firefighter, collapsed three steps out the door, a child in each arm. I am the corn in the field, the fruit on the vine, the meat on the bone. I am death that brings life; I give all for all. I am not the steady steed, the firm foundation – I am transaction, event, moment. Follow me if you follow my path!

ଓ   ଓ   ଓ   ଓ

Then the crowd split up and went to ten different areas, following each of the archetypes. The groups each concentrated on an activity related to that archetype. Group leaders had clocks, and each activity could take no more than an hour. Toward the end of the period, the wheel-pushers brought the wheel around to each group in turn, and they added items or energy to it. The canvas side with the ties had been attached, and people could tie their items to that side.

The Mad Scientist passed around the strange machine and told each group member to hold it, decide what sort of positive change could be made in the world by the right technology, and declare that this machine was that technology. Everyone then asked the Cosmos to bring that technology into being. When the wheel came around, they disassembled the machine and tied the pieces to it.

The Trickster held a discussion about what it is to be a real trickster that eventually degenerated into group joke-telling. One individual was voted Fool For A Day, and ceremoniously crowned with the silly hat.

The Rebel talked to his people about what rebellion really meant, especially responsible rebellion. They had a big sheet of plastic and some spray cans, and made magical graffiti to bring their goals. A piece of it was tied to the wheel.

Robin Hood's people were given artificial coins and told: *This is what you will take from those who don't need it, and give it to those who do, for this good purpose.* Then the coins were placed into a bag and tied to the wheel.

The Healer held a discussion group about what it was to be a Healer, and worked to lay on hands and heal each other. They were given pieces of rose quartz to charge and place into a bag. When the wheel came around, they tied the bag to it.

The Madwoman held a ritual of clarity and healing for all those who joined her due to their history of mental illness. They surrounded the wheel and wailed at it, to add their energy. The Monk led his people in a prayer and meditation, and then they made small prayer flags to string on a cord and tie to the wheel. The Artist got the blank canvas side of the wheel, and her people decorated it with a table full of paints, glitter, and other fast-drying art supplies; it was tied to the empty side of the wheel.

(We don't actually know what the Sexual Perverts did, as they went into a small room and closed the door, and the leader told us that it was all confidential. He did say that it all went very, very well. When the wheel came to them, they pulled it into the room, put it in their midst, and used vocal noises to raise energy and charge it.)

The Sacred King handed out a series of poems to his people gathered in a circle, and one poem chose the winner by lot. That one was chosen the new King, and given the horns. They spoke of sacrifice, and what it means to give of yourself. This group was the last to get the wheel, and their offering was to roll it down the hill to the fire circle, where a bonfire was burning.

ಲ ಲ ಲ ಲ

On the way out of the ritual space, when the wheel was ready to go, the participants passed between the elements and planets, each of whom blessed them in a different way, as follows:

East *(smudging people with incense)*: May your mind be blessed with clarity in the clouded times yet to come.

South *(waving fire fans)*: May your will be strong for the challenges yet to come.

West *(anointing with water)*: May your heart hold true through all the sadnesses yet to come.

North *(anointing with henna)*: May your body be healthy for the dancing yet to come.

Aquarius *(waving a fluorescent glowing wand)*: May inspiration flash in the dark moments yet to come.

Pisces *(waving an aqua glowing wand)*: May you understand when to sacrifice in the times yet to come.

Uranus *(waving a glittering wand)*: May you be open to all the changes yet to come.

Neptune *(waving a bubble wand)*: May all your dreams come to you.

Then the group processed to the fire. The Sacred King's group rolled the wheel, and the chosen King was the one to actually lay it on the fire. The tricksters danced around the procession. The monks brought up the rear, chanting solemnly. Everyone else found a place in between. At the fire, the canvases were removed and laid aside, and the wheel was burned, to much singing and cheering.

☙ ☙ ❧ ❧

The following day was the final ceremony. The two canvas circles were laid out on the ground, and many long yarn strings were tied to the outer-edge ties that had secured them to the wheel. The Officiant spoke, and took hold of the end of a thread. Each of the elements and planets spoke and took a thread as well.

☙ ☙ ❧ ❧

Officiant: We come together here and now on the longest day of the year to watch the year shift from waxing to waning. We come together to witness the magic that we have done, that binds us to the rest of the world and its changing tides.

East:
Hail to the summer winds that carry our wishes!
May you send our voices out into the world!
May you lend clarity to our messages,
That they might not be misunderstood.
May you get people thinking,
May you get minds churning,
May you bring new inspiration to humanity.
I take this thread, and I bless this coming summer
With new words that have never been spoken.

South:
Hail to the Sun on your longest day!
May you witness our works and be proud.
May you witness our joy and warm us.
May you get people moving,
May you chase away all apathy
With your fiery arms, with your fiery eyes.
I take this thread, and I bless this coming summer
With the fire to carry all our passions
Through the dullest times.

West:
>Hail to the waters that pound on every shore!
>May you run through our blood,
>May we taste you in our mouths,
>May we hear you beating in our ears,
>May we feel you when our hearts leap.
>I take this thread, and I bless this coming summer
>With the beauty of Love unconquered
>That breaks through all boundaries,
>That crosses all rivers,
>That turns all tides,
>That sails us home again.

North:
>Hail to the earth that blooms green beneath our feet!
>May you fill our bellies with nourishment,
>May you fill our eyes with beauty,
>May you hold firm beneath us
>And bear us up, even when we fall apart.
>May you remind us of the sacredness of our bodies.
>I take this thread, and I bless this coming summer
>With appreciation of the joy
>That is in embodied existence.

Uranus:
>Hail to the Power of Change that wings through our days!
>May we weather all change with grace,
>Or at least with good humor!
>May we welcome change with open arms,
>Or at least a sense of adventure!
>May we ride change like a wild horse
>Or at least not be trampled in the stampede!
>I take this thread, and I bless this coming summer
>With the unexpected, the bolt out of the blue,
>With victories that no one could possibly have predicted.

Neptune:
>Hail to the Power of Dreams that haunts our nights!
>May we keep believing in our dreams
>Even in the face of despair and defeat!
>May we hold onto our dreams
>Even in the face of those who scoff at them!
>May we let our dreams lead us to new worlds
>Where no map leads, and no path goes.
>I take this thread, and I bless this coming summer
>With the unimaginable force that brings people together
>In spite of all their differences,
>And binds us all in the greatest dream ever conceived
>In the never-ending womb of the Universe.

Officiant: Speak, and bless the coming year!

Each person, starting with the group leaders from the main ritual, came forth and took a thread and spoke a single word, denoting the quality with which they want to bless the coming year. This continued until the threads were all taken, and then the remaining people touched someone else's thread to speak their word. We made sure to include the quarter casters. When all were finished, the canvas wheels were rolled up like a bundle, and all the threads wrapped around them. The officiant blessed everyone present, and then the ritual was over.

Multicultural Solstice

We created this ritual as an example of contrasting Solstice rites; showing onlookers that rituals were different in northern and southern Europe, due to climatic changes. The ritual was both Babylonian- and Celtic-inspired, and requires the following staff and props:

- Four **Narrators**
- **Adonis**, dressed in golden robes
- **Mourning Mother**, dressed in black robes
- At least two **mourning women** in black or grey
- Two people with spears (or large tusks) to play the **Boar**
- **The Oak King**, dressed in brown with a wreath of oak leaves.
- **The Holly King**, dressed in green with a wreath of holly leaves.
- A **Servant**, to pass around slips of paper and pens for wagers, and collect them afterwards.
- **Singers**, who can be staff members or others
- A large red cloth, big enough to cover a person
- A basket
- A pot of nasturtiums – we grew them from seed in the spring for this purpose

First Narrator: Hail and well met! We come together on the longest day, where for thousands of years folk have come together before. We stand where our ancestors stood. Yet what was it that they did? The ancestors of our faith came from many different lands, and the Sun meant a different thing in each one. What is the Sun to you?

Shills in the audience call out "Life" or "Warmth" or whatever. Choir members begin to sing the following Mesopotamian chant low in the background.

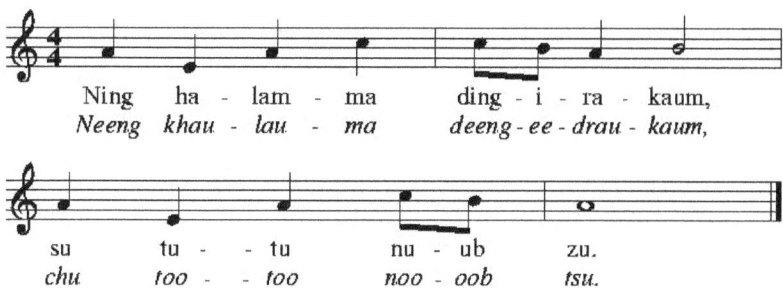

Second Narrator: In the hot countries of the Fertile Crescent, the height of the Solstice was not a time of joy and fertility. The Sun's wrath beat the last few crops into a burnt, dry powder. The delicate flowers withered and dried, and new planting would have to wait for the fall season when the summer's heat had declined. Here the Sun was Adonis – gentle youth, lover of the Great Goddess, felled by a ravening boar and doomed to have his blood spilled on the earth.

Adonis comes forward and stands with his back to the audience, his arms lifted skyward.

Third Narrator: In that time and place, small gardens were grown in pots on rooftops, called the Gardens of Adonis. They were set close to the sky, meeting the Sun, blooming with flowers in His colors ... and doomed to wither in the Solstice's heat.

First Narrator: Think of what you find beautiful that you know, in your heart, will never last. Think of what you find wonderful that must be enjoyed in the moment, while it lasts, for it will not last. Think of all that is fine and fleeting, and honor that in your heart. As the Mother bears the Garden of Adonis, take a flower and eat of it, and taste what you honor ... for these moments bring spice to our lives, but if we wait, they wither on the vine and are gone.

Mourning Mother walks around the circle offering the pot of nasturtiums to everyone. The final one is offered to the Sun King, who accepts it. As the Mother approaches the Sun King, the choir begins again the Mesopotamian chant, which gets louder and more ominous. He turns around, takes the flower and eats it, and then reaches out to touch the Mother. She reaches out for him as well, but at that moment he is speared from behind by the Boar people with two tusks. They should pass on either side of his torso. He falls, his fingers just missing hers. She stops, stricken, and falls to her knees.

First Narrator: Now think of a time when you risked, and you failed. Think of a time when you threw your heart into something, and you lost it. Perhaps it was a failure of will, or love, or courage. Perhaps it was just the way of the world, which thwarts even the Gods in their goals. Cry for that moment. Mourn that lost thing, especially if you have never truly mourned it before.

The Mother raises her eyes and screams and wails. The mourning women join in with her, and the choir sings the Mesopotamian chant very slowly and mournfully. They cover Adonis in sheer red cloth, and sprinkle ashes on him. The Mother and the mourners go about the circle brushing everyone with ashes, encouraging everyone to wail for their losses. Then the Mother comes to the bowl of water with the dipper and stops wailing. The mourners slowly quiet down.

Second Narrator: Yet with any loss, sorrow passes. Grief passes. Pain passes. Yet the hardest thing of all to let go of is often blame. We blame ourselves, or we blame others, or we blame the world. This too we must let go of, that Adonis may be buried, and next spring live anew.

Third Narrator: Will you come forth, each of you, and forgive, and be cleansed?

Each comes forth and the Mother asks them, "Who is to blame: yourself, or others, or the world?" Depending on how they answer, she asks, "Will you forgive yourself?" or "Will you forgive them?" or "Will you forgive the world?" If they answer yes, she pours water over their hands and says, "You are cleansed of blame," or "You are cleansed of anger," or "Trust in the world again."

ಌ   ಌ   ಌ   ಌ

Fourth Narrator: Many leagues away in a place wet and cold as Adon's bed was hot and dry, the Celtic peoples celebrated the Solstice as the changing of the year from the Oak King to the Holly King.

Second Narrator: Hail to the Oak King, Lord of the Waxing Year! Hail to you, strong as the stout beams of the oaken door, the oaken ship, the columns of the oaken pier, the enduring staff that helps us on your journey. Hail to the First Brother who is born at Yule, whose time is come at the height of the Summer!

The Oak King stands forth, in his brown tunic and wreath of oak leaves.

Third Narrator: Hail to the Holly King, Lord of the Waning Year! Hail to you, sharp as thorns and green even in the coldest winter, your red berries giving joy against the barren lands! Hail to the Second Brother who is born in Midsummer, whose time is come in the depths of Winter!

The Holly King stands forth, in a dark green tunic and wreath of holly leaves.

First Narrator: A battle is about to begin! Time to lay your bets – will it go well, or ill? There can be up to five rounds of fighting – on which round will the Oak King be slain? What will you wager? Will you wager your pride, or your fear of something, or a deed yet undone, or unfinished? Lay down your bets, Ladies and Gentlemen!

Drum sounds as people are given slips of paper to write what valuable thing they will wager, and perhaps lose. When that is done, the two kings fight. They can fight up to five rounds, but the two of them should decide beforehand how many they will fight and on which round their choreographed battle will end. At the beginning of the first round, and at the end of each consecutive round, they pause, and the First Narrator asks if there are more wagers to lay down. The servant with the basket collects them until the fight is over.

Fourth Narrator: Some will have won, some will have lost, for that is the way of Fortune. Give your markers to the Oak King, for in six months' time he will come to claim your debts, and they must be paid by then.

The Oak King rises and takes their debts in a bowl.

Oak King: In six months' time, then, I will come for you, and these will all be given over to me as birthing-gifts!

Holly King: I claim one token! *(Draws one randomly from the basket.)* This one is mine, and this will be claimed today! Come forth and give up your wager. *(The writer of that token comes forth and gives up what they had wagered.)*

First Narrator (call and response):
Hail to the height of the Sun!
Hail to the Sun's gifts,
Both generous and deadly!
Hail to all the ancestral paths,
From all corners of the world,
Where they watched the Sun rise
On the longest day
And praised its eternal rays.

Astrological Solstice Rite

This is the first of four astrological rites marking the main four quarters of the year, where one sign gives way to the other. In the case of the Solstice, Gemini (the sign of the Sacred Twins) gives way to Cancer (the sign of the Mother). This rite requires ten people, including three sets of mythical twins, three Mother figures, and one narrator. The parts are:

- **Narrator**, dressed in yellow like the Solstice Sun.
- **Castor**, dressed in a dark blue Grecian *chiton* and *himation*.
- **Pollux**, dressed in a sky-blue Grecian *chiton* and *himation*.
- **Demeter**, dressed in a green *chiton* and wheat-gold *himation*.
- **Helen**, dressed in a *chiton* and *himation* of glittering rose and gold, with dramatic makeup, flowers in her hair, and lots of jewelry.
- **Clytemnestra**, dressed in a grey *chiton* with a purple *himation*, and a black veil on her head.
- **Gaea**, dressed in draped cloth of all the colors of the Earth. Alternately, she can be naked with body paint.
- **Shachar**, the Canaanite god of Dawn, dressed in a long Syrian tunic of sunrise colors.
- **Shalim**, the Canaanite god of Dusk, dressed in a long Syrian tunic of sunset and twilight colors.
- **Asherah**, the Canaanite Mother Goddess, dressed in a long Syrian tunic of red, with a *shatwih* headdress with the moon on the front of it.

A note on costuming: It's not hard to find pictures of ancient Greek clothing, but young men usually wore a *chiton*, or short tunic made from a tube of fabric folded over at the top in a flange, and secured at the shoulders with brooches; and a short knee-length cloak (the *himation*) made from a single length of cloth, secured over one shoulder. A woman's *chiton* was of the same shape but ankle-length, and her *himation* would also be floor-length. Both sexes wore tied girdles or belts, and women might wear the X-shaped cord across their chests, dividing their breasts and giving support. Some wore a second X-shape around the midriff.

Canaanites of both genders wore what is referred to modernly as the "Syrian tunic"; if you can find the Folkwear patterns for the "Gaza Dress" or "Syrian Dress", you can get a good idea of what they looked like: an A-shaped, long-sleeved, often heavily embroidered caftan-style gown still worn as traditional clothing in many places in the Middle East. The *shatwih* female headdress is an 8" truncated cone-hat – much like a slightly taller version of the modern male *fez* – over which an elaborately trimmed veil is draped and pinned.

Each "twin" in this ritual should carry a double-edged blade, either a knife or a sword. In addition, Castor and Pollux carry a bowl of grain (we used millet), Shachar and Shalim carry a cup of honey, and Helen and Clytemnestra carry a cup of salt water.

The Narrator's robe can match the Greek or the Canaanite theme, as people desire.

ଔ   ଔ   ଟ   ଟ

First the ritual staff takes their places. The Narrator stands in the center. Demeter, Gaea, and Asherah stand in the North. Castor and Pollux stand in the East, Shachar and Shalim in the South, Helen and Clytemnestra in the West. The Narrator speaks first.

Narrator: We hail the Sun on the longest day of the year, and also we hail the Sun's path through the sacred Signs of the Sky. For the last turn of the Moon, the Sun has been in the sign of the Holy Twins. There are many sets of Holy Twins in the world, but today we will honor three of them. The Sun is about to pass into the sign of Cancer, the Mother and Child, the place of home and family. We hail the Sun's presence as it passes!

Shachar and Shalim raise their arms to the southern sky.

Shachar: Hail to the Spirits of the South, on this day when the Sun rises here!

Shalim: Hail to the Spirits of Fire, who give us energy, and light up the world so that we can see clearly!

All: Hail!

Helen and Clytemnestra lift their arms to the western sky.

Helen: Hail to the Spirits of the West, of the heart that beats with love.

Clytemnestra: Hail to the Spirits of Water, who pour from our eyes when we weep salt tears of sorrow.

All: Hail!

The Narrator speaks for the North, holding arms up to the northern sky.

Narrator: Hail to the Spirits of the North, of the body that warms with the Sun's touch! Hail to the Spirits of Earth, the ground under our feet!

All: Hail!

Castor and Pollux lift their arms to the eastern sky.

Castor: Hail to the Spirits of the East, of the two-edged blade that is our inheritance – of thought and of strife!

Pollux: Hail to the Spirits of Air, of the mind that opens to all possibilities!

All: Hail!

Castor: I am Castor, a prince of ancient Greece. My father was King Tyndareus, and my mother was Queen Leda. From birth, I and my twin brother Pollux loved each other more than anyone. We were brothers and shieldmates forever ... until Fate caused my death.

Pollux: I am Pollux, the son of Queen Leda, who was also the son of the great god Zeus. Half-immortal, I could not go to Hades with my brother, so when he died, I cried to Zeus for justice. He made us a bargain: if I sacrificed my life and half my immortality, we could spend half our time in Hades, and half on Olympus, always together.

Castor: So it was done! And so we remain together, proof that two can share one destiny – if they remain bound together by love.

Pollux: Let your heart and your mind be bound together by love, rather than fighting each other. Here we pass our love, grown like the grain from the seeds we planted together, to the Mother of the Fields. Hail to you, Mother!

Demeter comes forth and the Twins give her the bowl of grain. She kisses them both.

Demeter: Blessings upon you, and your love and loyalty. I will take this grain into my time on the Earth, and scatter them to the winds, that they may choose their place to grow. As you came from a Mother, so may you go with a Mother's love.

Next, Shachar and Shalim get the group's attention.

Shachar: I am Shachar, the Sacred Twin of Dawn! I am the First Gatekeeper, the moment when you awaken to a new day. I bring you all good news: if you are still alive, you have one more chance to learn what you have not yet learned, to do what you should have done yesterday, to make yet one more small difference in the world.

Shalim: I am Shalim, the Sacred Twin of Dusk! I am the Second Gatekeeper, the moment when you realize that the day is over, and appraise what you have done and left undone. I bring you all a painful reminder: some may not live to see tomorrow, so do not put off what can be done today! Have you told those you care for how much you care for them? Do not forget it!

Shachar: I am the optimism of morning, and you need me, if you are to keep from losing hope. My brother and I are points of balance, and we understand each other.

Shalim: I am the assessment of evening, and you need me as well, even if I find you wanting. Here we pass our hope and memories, sweet as honey, to the Mother who bore us. Hail to you, Mother!

Asherah comes forth and the Twins give her the cup of honey. She kisses them both.

Asherah: Blessings upon you, and your keen senses of both hope and caution. I will take this honey and sweeten the minds of humanity that they may know both hope and reward for their work. As you came from a Mother, so may you go with a Mother's love.

Next, Helen and Clytemnestra get the group's attention.

Helen: I am Helen of Troy, or so they call me, the sister of Castor and Pollux. Like my brother Pollux, I am the daughter of the great god Zeus, and my beauty was so legendary that kings fought over me. Unlike my brothers, I scorned my plain and mortal sister Clytemnestra, leaving her to be the pawn of powerful men while I enjoyed my privilege. I was Light, and she was Darkness, and I had no use for her, no use at all.

Clytemnestra: I am Clytemnestra, and I am merely the daughter of Tyndareus and Leda. I was sold into marriage, again and again, imprisoned, my children taken from me and killed, and no one cared. But when those powerful men turned their backs, I had my revenge. I took allies, I chose my own lover, I turned their laws upside down and killed them in their own bathtubs. That which you ignore and abuse, that which you lock away in contempt, can rise up against you, and she has the right to do so!

Helen: In the final chapter of the story, we both came to a bad end – I torn apart by the widows of dead soldiers, angry with the war I'd started with my infidelities and foolishness; you slain by the son that you ignored as you were ignored. Light and dark, we lost because we lost each other. We stand here as a lesson: honor both sides, or be destroyed.

Clytemnestra: Learn from our mistakes! Do not do as we have done! If you are divided within yourself – mind and heart, judgment and appetite, desire and common sense – build a bridge between the parts of your soul! Find a way to bring them together, or all hope is lost. Here we pass the cup of salt water, our shared tears, to the Mother who received our bodies. Hail to you, Mother!

Gaea comes forth and the Twins give her the cup of salt water. She pours it out onto the ground and brings them both into her embrace.

Gaea: Blessings upon you, my suffering children. I will hold you in my body and my heart, and bring you peace. I will water the whole Earth with your tears, that all may know your tale and understand it in themselves. As you came from a Mother, so may you go with a Mother's love.

The Narrator stands forth from the North and speaks again.

Narrator: Mothers who watch and love, who dry our tears, who feed our bodies, will you give take charge of the next part of the Sun's cycle?

Demeter: We will, and we will help you to create loving bonds and a peaceful home.

Asherah: We will, and we will help you to remember your own family, by blood or by choice, and to say the things that should be not left unsaid.

Gaea: We will, and we will help you to remember the Mother beneath your feet, who gives so much to you.

Narrator: Thank you for your blessings! Farewell to the Sacred Twins; your time will come again next year. Welcome to the Mothers – we were all born of mothers once!

All: Hail!

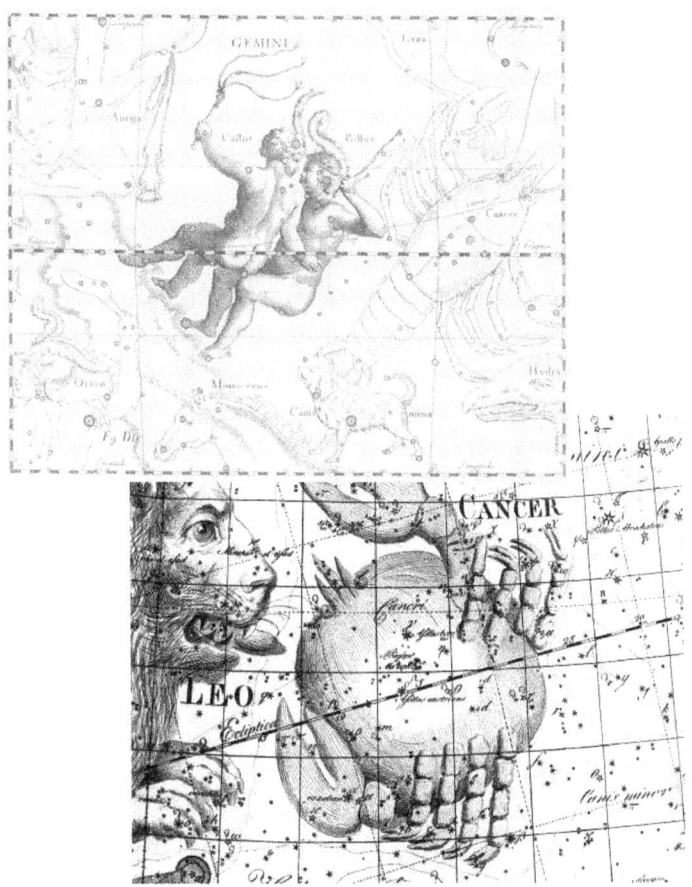

Romanized Harvest Ritual

The Mediterranean Roman climatic year was such that their harvest rites were not covalent with the Northern European Lammas-through-Mabon harvest season, but this ritual can be used for any harvest festival. We have used it for Mabon, but it is not specific to any given month, only to a time of gathering in food.

Four women stand at the four quarters of the circle, in Roman garb. The woman in the North wears a green robe, a wreath of leaves, and carries a leafy branch; the woman in the West wears a golden robe, a crown of grain and bears a sheaf of grain; the woman in the South wears a red robe, a simple brown headscarf, and bears a torch (or at least a lit candle in a jar); the woman in the East wears a yellow robe, a crown of fruits and/or vegetables, and carries a basket of the fruits of the harvest. To the side stands a man in a black toga and a heavy gold chain, carrying a scythe.

An officiant stands forth in Roman garb, followed by two assistants in Roman tunics. One carries a large urn of water with flower petals in it and a towel, and the other carries a censer of incense. The officiant carries a vial of blessed oil with appropriate essential oils in it – cypress, frankincense, myrrh, etc. He calls out: *"Purificatio!"* and the three of them make the rounds of the circle of people. All have their hands washed ceremoniously, are censed with incense, and are marked on the head with sacred oil.

ॐ ॐ ॐ ॐ

Officiant: Hail to all those present, and to all the Gods, and to the mighty fecund Earth below us! Tellus Mater, bless us today, for from you we all sprang and to you we will all return.

The woman in the North stands forward.

Tellus Mater: The Earth welcomes and blesses you, my children. Long before you tilled the soil and bred the trees and animals, you lived from my breast. This is my blessing: May food be always there when you need it; may you never starve from lack of plenty, be it your own table or that of others. For I provide for all my children, if they have eyes to see or hands to gather or loved ones to take the place of eyes and hands.

She walks around the circle and brushes them with the tree branch.

Officiant: Hail to Tellus Mater! *(All shout "Hail!")* Hail to the crops that grow on the Earth, whose grains we sow and who give us back thousands more! Ceres, Grain Mother, bless us today, for you fill our bellies and filled those of our ancestors.

The woman in the West stands forward.

Ceres: The fertile fields welcome and bless you, my children. Once, long ago, you turned from simply hunting and gathering to placing seeds in soil and cultivating the new plants against all odds. You thrived on this new skill, and you created new plants that had never been seen before. You learned to partner with the Earth, instead of simply taking like children. Now your bellies are filled every day with the food that the Earth gives you, but that you also work to produce. But remember that in a partnership, you must give back as much as you take, and give back things of lasting value. May you be nourished!

She walks around the circle and brushes them with the sheaf of grain.

Officiant: Hail to Ceres! *(All shout "Hail!")* Hail to the crops that are harvested and prepared for our food! Ops Consiva, Lady of the Granary, bless us today, for you help to feed us for the future.

The woman in the East stands forward.

Ops: Once you had food from the fields, you prospered and grew in numbers ... and then you realized that even when the season was not right, you could save the food you had harvested and feed hundreds. You learned to dry, and preserve, and plan. You learned that for every seed you harvested, you had to save another to put back into the Earth and guarantee next year's harvest. You learned to work together, in large groups, in villages, in towns. You learned to live together in large groups as well. But now you must remember that the Earth needs balance, and your nourishment must be balanced with the future. May your futures teach you well!

She walks around the circle and touches one of the fruits in her basket to people's heads.

Officiant: Hail to Ops! *(All shout "Hail!")* Hail to the food that is brought into the house every year, prepared, counted, saved, and which bears the hopes of every householder for survival in the winter. Hestia Tamia, Lady of the Pantry, bless us today, for you see to it that no one starves at the table.

The woman in the South stands forward.

Hestia Tamia: I am the one who counts every sack, every cup of milk, every cheese and piece of meat. I am the one who carefully puts aside each sack of flour and each piece of meat, who adds up the hay for the animals kept through the winter and decides how many can live. I am the one who asks you to sacrifice to me, and to sacrifice to me is to let the weary stranger in the door for dinner, even when there is little enough to feed all at the table. I am the one who makes sure that no one goes hungry because someone was careless. May your hearths be warm and comforting, and may your tables be full forever. Warm your busy hands at my fire.

She walks around the circle with the candle, inviting each one to warm their hands over her lit candle.

Officiant: Hail to Hestia Tamia! *(All shout "Hail!")* Hail to the goddesses of the land that feeds us. May we keep their gifts in the heart of our homes.

Officiant brings out a bowl of whole grains, and everyone takes a handful. They can throw it into the fire, or to the birds, or take it home to keep – all feeds some spirit, and thus it is sacred.

Astrological Mabon Ritual

This rite celebrates the Autumn Equinox and the turning of the solar year astrologically from Virgo to Libra. It requires eight participants, four of whom represent archetypes of Virgo and four for archetypes of Libra.

- **The Virgin Maiden** (or Virgin Youth, if you want to be gender-nonconformist). Using a young girl or boy just past puberty who is more likely to be an actual virgin can work, or someone can be virgin in spirit. Doing a private purificatory rite beforehand can help them to keep the mindset. The Virgin wears a simple white shift or tunic and holds a stick with ribbons.

- **The Monk.** While monks tend to be associated with Christianity or Buddhism or Hinduism, there were cloistered holy people in ancient times (especially in urban areas like Rome); the modern Catholic monastic hours are based on the earlier Hellenic sacred priestly hours which performed the same function for Pagan monastics. In modern Neo-Paganism, some folk are beginning to create monastic paths and cloistered groups based in our various faiths, so the Monk doesn't have to look Catholic, Buddhist, or Hindu. We put him in a green robe with bare feet, a stick, and a wreath of greenery.

- **The Harvest Queen.** Dressed in harvest colors (our Harvest Queen had a gown patchworked of various autumn-leaf quilting fabrics), the Harvest Queen bears a sheaf of grain or a cornucopia full of vegetables.

- **The Spinner.** An elderly woman in grey, brown, or black with a drop spindle, which she keeps spinning as she speaks. If she can actually hand-spin, that would be best, but if not it's best to wind the spindle with many pieces of already-spun yarn that she can unwind, and attach one piece to the hook at the top that she can spin back and forth. If an actual spinning wheel can be brought out as a prop, so much the better.

- **The Dancer, or Artist.** Either archetype works. Dressed in festive, fanciful clothing, the Dancer or Artist spills glitter and butterflies everywhere. Can be any gender.

- **The White Knight/Black Knight.** A warrior dressed half in white and half in black, he goes back and forth from being the idealist to being the challenger. He/she carries a cup and a sword.

- **The Lover.** This can be played by a person of either gender. They dress in light colors and carry flowers.

- **The Judge.** Dressed in a severe black robe and carrying a heavy-looking scepter, the Judge is serious and never smiles.

The eight staff members file in, the first four from one direction (the Virgo team) and the second four from the other direction (the Libra team). The two groups stand facing each other across the central space, then the Libra team steps back and the Virgo team moves to stand the four directions. The Maiden/Youth takes the East, the Monk takes the South, the Spinner takes the West, and the Harvest Queen the north.

Maiden/Youth:

Hail to the Spirits of the East!
Hail to the Autumn sunrise!
Renew us with each breath
And help us to find newness in the old.
May we keep our minds sharp
And our words clean and precise.

Monk:

Hail to the Spirits of the South!
Hail to the Autumn noontime!
Give us patience to walk each step

Of the road that is set before us.
Give us patience to toil in the Sun
So that we may set food before our brothers.

Spinner:

Hail to the Spirits of the West!
Hail to the Autumn sunset!
May we look into the deep well of twilight
And of mystery, and may it all make sense.
May we wind our emotions up in the string
Of self-control, and not let spill our wrath.

Harvest Queen:

Hail to the Spirits of the North!
Hail to the Autumn nights!
Give us bounty in our harvests
And may there be enough for all.
May we cherish every grain and nut,
Every fruit and green thing of the Mother beneath us.

One of the staff members then stands forward to narrate. This can be one of the existing eight (we used the Judge) or you can choose a separate narrator.

Narrator: Welcome to the Reckoning Day, the second point in the year when Day and Night are equal. This day comes near to the end of the harvest season in many places on the northern third of this world, and did so for many of our ancestors as well. Also, this day marks the change when the Sun above us moves from Virgo, the sign of the Virgin, ruled by Mercury, to Libra, the sign of the Scales, ruled by Venus.

Virgo is a sign of Earth, of Practicality, of Work and Labor, of Service, of Attention to Detail, of Numbers, of Restraint, of Privacy. This is the time of Counting, of tallying up the fruits of one's labor so that you may know how you did for the year. It is represented here by the

Virgin Maiden in her self-enclosed bower, the Monk in his cloister, the Spinner bent over her wheel, and the Harvest Queen who holds all we have toiled to earn.

Libra is a sign of Air, of Idealism, of Two Sides To Every Question. One side of Libra's scales desires Love and Harmony and Art and the delights of Venus. The other side desires Justice at all costs. We now face the time where we must decide where to allocate the resources we painstakingly gathered during Virgo's reign. With whom will you share your harvest? Will there be enough, for yourself and others? Into which side of the scales will you lay your year's work? These are the decisions that come to us at this moment. To aid us in this, Libra is represented here by the Dancer (or Artist), the White Knight who is also the Black Knight, the Lover, and the Judge.

However, for the moment, Virgo holds the ground. As the Virgin's sign prepares to leave the field, listen well to their wisdom, for it will not come around again until next year's harvest.

The Virgin Maiden turns to the people.

Virgin Maiden:

Equal Day and Equal Night!
I stand in the place between innocence
And knowing the wider world.
I am enclosed behind the high wall of the garden
Because sometimes the soul needs a quiet place to grow.
Have you all given yourselves time to be alone,
To let your wounds heal in solitude,
To recover from the demands of others?
Or have you starved yourself for that inner peace?
Have you set good boundaries between yourself and others
Or do you always let them invade your garden?
Come to me for the gift of solitude of the soul.

Those who wish shall come forward, and the Virgin Maiden gives them each a white piece of cloth, telling them to bind it around their heads when they want privacy and solitude.

Then the Monk comes forward.

Monk:
>Equal Day and Equal Night!
>I stand in the place between serving the people
>And serving the Gods and their Divine Will.
>I am cloistered away from the world,
>But I am not lonely, for prayer is my friend,
>And the Gods are my solace.
>I come out only to give service to those in need.
>Have you given service to others lately?
>Have you given service to the Gods?
>Come make your promises to both, if you would be blessed.

Those who wish shall come forward, and the Monk shall give them many ribbons, which they shall tie onto his staff. Some are plain, for service to humanity; some are shining for service to the Gods.

Then the Spinner comes forward.

Spinner:
>Equal Day and Equal Night!
>I stand in the place between thoughtless labor and mindful work,
>Always searching for perfection in crafting.
>I am the one who knows how to work on into the night,
>Who sees every detail and hones each skill.
>Are you laboring, or are you lazy?
>Are you doing a good job, or are you careless?
>Is your skill polished, or do you need more practice?
>If you would have patience to reap your harvest
>And the conscientiousness to do it well,
>Come to me for the gift of honorable labor.

Those who wish shall come forward, and the Spinner shall give them a bit of yarn from her spindle, and tell them, "Be a better craftsman."

Then the Harvest Queen comes forward.

Harvest Queen:
    Equal Day and Equal Night!
    I stand in the place between hunger and plenty,
    Feeding those with empty bellies,
    Measuring out each grain to make sure
    That it will go as far as possible.
    Have you reaped enough this year to survive?
    Have you reaped enough to share with others?
    Are you willing to divide the bread a little thinner
    To feed those in need?
    If so, come forth and take my blessing
    That you may survive the winter with enough for all,
    That you may have bounty in future years.

Those who wish shall come forward, and the Harvest Queen shall bless them with a touch on the belly, saying, "Full and content, always." Then all four of the Virgo Team steps back, and the Libra Team comes in, taking their places. The Dancer goes to the East, the Knight goes to the South, the Lover goes to the West, and the Judge goes to the North.

Narrator: And now the Virgin's Sun steps aside, and the Scales take their turn in the fields. We go from measuring to allocating, from our own pantries to those of the greater world.

Dancer:
    Equal Day and Equal Night!
    I stand in the place between what we see in our minds
    And what our bodies and wills can make manifest!
    I am the dance that is imagined and then carried out!
    I am the art that is created, the vision made real!
    Have you been practicing the art that you love?
    Does your creativity flow freely, or is it dammed up?
    If you would bring forth your art more easily,

Come to me and I will bless you!

Those who wish shall come forward, and the Dancer shall dance with each of them in some way for a moment.

Then the Knight comes forward.

White Knight/Black Knight:
Equal Day and Equal Night!
I stand in the place between the holy grail of the shining ideal
And the sword of the adversary who opposes you!
Are you the gentle one who strives to help others,
Or are you the suspicious one who waylays your enemies?
Or are you sometimes both? I know that it is hard
To be the White Knight and not lapse into the Black.
If you would keep from seeing enemies everywhere,
But still be able to defend yourself when necessary.
Come to me for the blessing of compassionate objectivity.

Those who wish shall come forward, and the White Knight shall ask them whether they are too much the idealist or too much the suspicious challenger. If the former, he gives them a sip from the cup; if the latter, he touches them with the sword.

Then the Lover comes forth.

Lover:
Equal Day and Equal Night!
I stand in the place between the ideal of romantic love
And the reality of what it takes to be in relationship.
I am the one who knows how to compromise,
Who learns what it is to be more attached to another
Than to your own insecurities and fears.
Have you found the balance point between real and ideal Love?
What flowers of love did you plant in others' fields?
What harvest have you reaped in your relationships?
If you would find love, or nourish love you already have,
Come to me and answer these questions,

And receive the blessing of Venus.

Those who wish shall come forward, and the Lover shall give each of them a flower.

Then the Judge steps forth.

Judge:
　　Equal Day and Equal Night!
　　I stand in the place between what this one says
　　And what that one says,
　　What is right for one and what is right for all.
　　I am the one who make the hard decisions
　　About who wins and who loses,
　　Who is freed and who is punished.
　　Do you have trouble judging those around you?
　　Do you err on the side of leniency or sternness?
　　Do you have trouble judging yourself and your actions?
　　Is there no justice in your life?
　　If you would have this fairness, come to me
　　For the gift of the Scales that balance.

The Judge walks slowly around the circle. He asks each person, "What trial have you faced this year, and what did you do about it?" When they speak, he tells them either, "You have done what you can; rest from it now," or "Not enough. There is more that you must do." This can be discerned by the Judge carrying two small stones of different shapes and colors in a bag; as each person speaks he draws a stone to divine what they must do. When he has walked all around the circle, he returns to the North and the Libra team dismisses the elements.

Dancer:
　　We thank you, Spirits of the East,
　　Powers of the Winds that blow!
　　May you infuse our speech with fantasy
　　That we may tell beautiful stories to each other!
　　May we dance with the autumn dawn
　　And revel in its beauty.

White Knight/Black Knight:

> We thank you, Spirits of the South,
> Powers of the Fire that energizes us!
> May you show us the road of rightness
> And also, that it is sometimes more than one road.
> Give us the torch of our hopes to carry
> And may it light our way.

Lover:

> We thank you, Spirits of the West,
> Powers of the Waters that flow.
> May you open our hearts to harmony
> And show us the divine in each of us.
> May we all be beautiful in each others' eyes,
> If only for a moment.

Judge:

> We thank you, Spirits of the North,
> Powers of the Earth like bedrock beneath us.
> May you show us all sides of the mountain,
> And the many different roads to the top.
> May you hold us to our commitments
> Even in the face of inconvenience and difficulty.
> Hail to the Equal Day and Equal Night!
> Hail to the turning of the Sun!

All shout "Hail" and the rite is over.

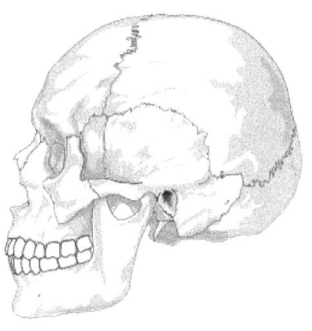

Samhain Rituals

Samhain Rites: The Wide Game

Samhain is our second largest ritual of the year. For our Samhain rites, we use a concept called the "wide game". I learned this term in Scouting, as a child; a wide game was a series of "stations", usually in the woods or along a trail, each with a different activity. Groups of people go from station to station, sometimes singly, sometimes in a trickle, sometimes in larger numbers. Some stations might simply act something out, some might require an activity, some might give people a choice which may reverberate later into their experiences at different stations.

Obviously, for wide game rituals you need either a large piece of property (ideally with clear paths, especially as Samhain rites often happen at night) or a building with a number of large rooms on different levels. Some rites require that the various stations be out of earshot of each other. This is sometimes because it will ruin the surprise of people at the last station, but also because it is distracting to be hearing other groups doing their invocations or questioning or other activities.

Wide game rituals are excellent for theatrical rituals and teaching people about what it is like to "walk through a story", but unlike "stage" rituals, the people at each station are on their own with a group of restless people, and need to be responsible and on their game. During one ritual, the staff member at the first gate decided to change the number of people allowed through at a time, and how long they would wait between groups. This ended up throwing the timing of every other station into disarray. More so than with circle rites, wide games need to be rehearsed and walked through so that everyone can get an accurate idea of how long they have with each group.

The other problem with wide game rites is that unless everyone in the group goes together from station to station, you will have some people finishing first and hanging around while the others catch up. This almost blew away one rite for us – the Egyptian underworld rite – because it was written with the assumption of perhaps forty people, and we got twice that many.

A huge drift of people who had already gone through the stations piled up around the bonfire where they had been told to wait, and their noise began to interfere with the stations. Some quick-witted folks stepped in and began to tell Egyptian stories with lots of entertaining voice and hand gestures, and another staff member broke out the cider they had brought for potluck and heated it on the fire, passing it out in small cupfuls to all the shivering participants.

The ritual was saved, but it was a serious realization for us: large groups of people cannot be left to mill about for half an hour or more in the cold. Someone should be assigned to each "waiting" group; sometimes they can be told to quietly meditate and will do so, but that usually breaks down with more than half a dozen people. Those who have nothing to do but wait should have someone assigned to do some kind of meaningful activity with them.

Depending on your climate, Samhain can also be very cold. Here in New England, we've had a couple of Samhains where it was cold enough for a snow flurry or two. Long, drawn-out rituals should be evaluated for chill factor – how long can people walk around in the cold and the dark? Having someone to make sure that the after-ritual potluck contains lots of hot food and drink helps as well.

At Asphodel, our Samhain rites – like our Beltane rites – have one part that we do every year, and that everyone expects. That is the Feast for the Dead which ends every rite, regardless of what the first half has been like. A table is set up with good cloths, china, candles, fall decorations, and a few tasteful skulls and glass balls scattered about. At some point in the ritual, we segue into pulling back the curtains we've rigged to hide the feast table, and then everyone surrounds it and names the names of their beloved Dead. Food and other offerings are laid on the table for the Dead, and libations are poured for them. The choir sings appropriate songs. Sometimes we have been able to dry a stash of roses over the year, which are given out to the attendees to take to the bonfire and burn for the Dead. This means that all the Samhain rituals given here have no real closure, because they always end in this rite. If this isn't something that your group is interested in doing, we encourage you to come up with your own ritual closure.

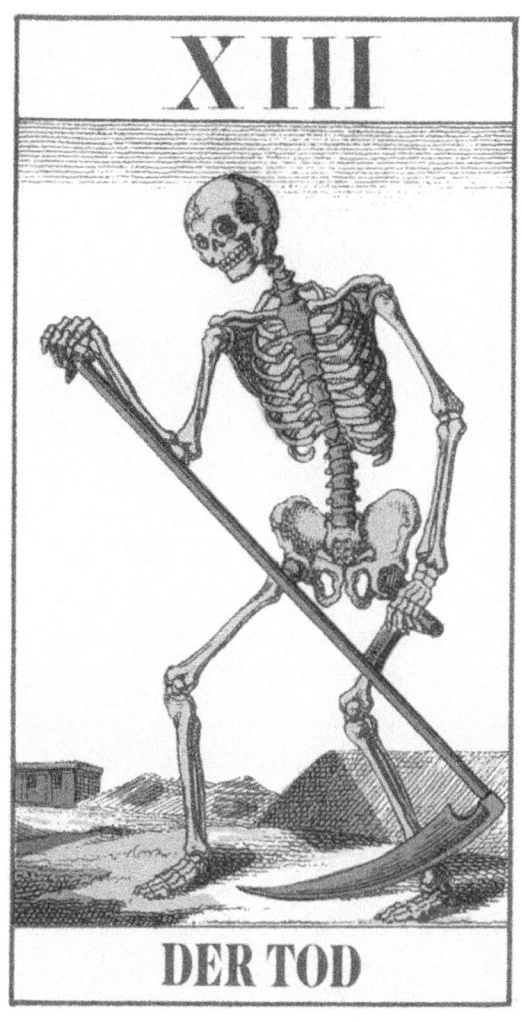

Egyptian Samhain

This was the first of our series of Samhain rituals that brought people to different cosmological Underworlds. It was created and run by Ana Anpuhemet; she was good enough to give me the outline of the ritual to reproduce here. The ritual comprises a journey to the Egyptian Underworld. It can be done in shifts if there is a very large group of people, or as one group if there are less than 25 non-staff participants. Know your groups and use your judgment – if there is likely to be restless behavior should people get bored waiting for the rite to end, have alternate activities waiting for them.

Characters should be in Egyptian garb with appropriate headdresses, if possible. Scrutinize ancient Egyptian pictures of the Gods – there are plenty to choose from. One problem that we ran into was doing a ritual from a hot-climate, scantily-clad culture during October in a cold region of the world; this was solved by wearing close-fitting clothing in medium-to-dark skin tones over long underwear and under the Egyptian *schenti* (kilts) and *kalasiris* (dresses). The traditional decorative collars and bracelets are great for concealing necklines and cuffs of modern clothing.

The names of the Gods in this ritual are spelled out in their original ancient Egyptian versions, rather than the Hellenized versions that we are used to in modern times. Whether you want to use the authentic names or the more familiar ones will, again, depend on your audience and what is likely to confuse them.

Participants in the rite should be told to bring a small item – something that can fit in the palm of the hand – that is personal to them, and possibly symbolic of something important to their lives. Of course, if this is a large public ritual, not everyone will hear about or remember this request, and alternatives will be explained to them just in case – a bit of hair or fingernail paring, house keys, iPods, or other items that are often used in people's lives.

The ritual requires the following staff members:

- **Greeter:** Can be dressed in Egyptian costume or not, as you like. Greeter has responsibility for briefing everyone about what will be expected of them.

- **Aset (Isis):** Queen of the Gods and wife of Osiris, she is one of the four guides of the Dead, and specifically the one who guides upper-class important people, those of wealth and power. In a small group, this would include not only those with wealth and power in the "ordinary" world, but people of great influence in the group itself. Isis wears pure white and her headdress bears colorful wings. If you can craft fabric wings the length of her arms, even better. She wears an elaborately tied girdle that is her other symbol.

- **Nebet Het (Nephthys):** Sister of Isis, wife of Set, and mother of Anubis, she wears grey and guides the working-class Dead, those who work hard to support themselves and their families, but would not be called wealthy or influential. Her symbol is the winnowing basket.

- **Neith:** Warrior and huntress, she wears red and guides the Dead who are warrior-types. Her symbol is a spear.

- **Selket:** Wearing bronze and a scorpion on her head, Selket guides the "outcasts" of society, and also those with great darkness on their souls. Her symbol is a staff, also with a scorpion on top.

- **Ma'at:** The goddess of Justice, she wears white with fabric wings of black and gold. She will need a large and impressive set of scales at her final station; we crafted a theatrical set that would shift to one side or the other at the touch of an unobtrusive lever, rather than responding to what was actually in their trays. She has two bowls at her station. One contains an even number of black and white stones; one contains a dozen or so hieroglyphs drawn on markers, each symbolizing a particular personal quality. These bowls are both used for divination on the spot.

- **The *Nun*:** This is someone of any gender representing the darkness of the Void. *Nun* (pronounced "noon") means the dark void, and this staff member is entirely swathed in black – just a walking sheet of darkness.

- **Het Her (Hathor):** Usually thought of as the goddess of love, Het Her supposedly lived in a small house on the way to the Underworld, and when Dead souls passed by it, she gave them food and water. She wears red, of a darker red than Neith's, and has a bowl of small ceramic scarabs and a bowl of oil.

- **Anpu (Anubis):** The jackal-headed psychopomp god, Anpu wears black underclothing and a black jackal-head mask, with a white *schenti* and gold jewelry. He carries a gold staff with which to herd people along.

- **Tehuti (Thoth):** The divine scribe, his job is to record all that happens in the Underworld. Dressed in light blue and white, he wears an ibis-head headdress and carries a piece of papyrus and a reed pen.

- **Heru (Horus):** The son of Isis and Osiris, his headdress is that of a hawk, and he wears lapis-blue and gold with the symbol of the *Udjat* eye covering one of his eyes.

- **Asar (Osiris):** The Lord of the Underworld, he sits on a throne with his body wrapped in white sheeting like that of a mummy. His arms are wrapped crossing his body with his green-gloved hands protruding, holding the sacred crook and flail. His face is colored green, and he wears his traditional white headdress. The man who plays Asar needs to be well-spoken and quick-thinking, as it will be his job to say appropriate things to the people who come before him.

- **Asar's Attendant:** This is someone dressed in Egyptian garb who stands next to the throne of Asar, and leads the participants away to the waiting area after they have been spoken to by him. Since the staff member playing Asar has very limited mobility, the attendant is also in charge of assisting him – holding water to his lips if he needs it, adjusting the costume, picking up things he may drop, etc. Asar's assistant also holds a bowl of hieroglyphic markers, several of them with good symbols and one with a bad symbol; the assistant will discreetly and randomly pull one marker for each person and show it to Asar as a divination.

- **Ammut:** The Monster who devours unworthy hearts. Ammut can look like the traditional fanged hippo, or it can be a monster of any sort you like – there are plenty of grotesque masks in the stores around Samhain. Ammut never speaks, but merely devours the "hearts" that are thrown to him, loudly and animalistically. The more dramatically this is done, the better.

The stations and props are as follows:

- **Entry and gathering-room.** This can be the driveway, the beginning point of a path in the woods, the gathering-room of a building, etc. No need for any props except perhaps chairs and places to hang coats if the rite is to be inside. Greeter stays here and waits to be cued by the entry of the four goddesses, and then follows the group through the ritual.

- **Gate to the Underworld.** This can be marked by a curtain or just a piece of black fabric stretched across a path, just short of the next area. At this station, everyone is given a small pouch of fabric with the Egyptian hieroglyph for "heart" painted on it.

- **Opening of the Mouth area.** Here there are two rows of chairs, back to back. Props needed here are two bowls of water, two cups of myrrh-scented oil (each containing a feather to touch people with), two incense holders with incense, and two sacred knives set on a small table. In a basket lays a pile of veils made from very thin, sheer fabric.

- **Het Her's house.** Ideally this is either a little room (or an area of a larger room) draped with fabric like a tent, or a small tent if this ritual is done outside. She has a couch and table with food and drink set out on it.

- **Hall of Judgment.** This area has Ma'at's scale, and Ammut waits crouched by it. It should be tall and dramatic, if possible, with walls covered in Egyptian paintings of the Gods. (We painted them on canvas and hung them up.)

- **Throne Room of Osiris.** This area has a throne for Osiris, and any other grand decoration that you want to give him.

- **Bonfire area.** This is a place of warmth and low lighting where people wait after their turn. We did this ritual outside and used a bonfire with benches and mats around it, but a candlelit room with plenty of comfortable seating will work as well. There should be some amount of food and drink here; if you want to be authentic you can make ancient Egyptian recipes for people to taste.

- **The Heart of *Nun*.** This is a room with seating on the floor in a circle (with perhaps a chair or two for those who cannot make it to the floor for physical reasons) lit only by a single candle.

‧ ‧ ‧ ‧

The participants are gathered at the entry point and the Greeter waits with them. At the appointed time, the goddesses Aset, Nebet Het, Neith, and Selket appear, and the Greeter says:

Greeter: Welcome, honored guests, to this year's Samhain celebration; Sekhet Aaru – the Egyptian Underworld.

During this ritual, you will cross to the Land of the Dead as you cross the river Aaru. As you reach the western bank, you will be handed an "ab" or heart pouch to put your personal trinkets in, and this will represent your heart that will be weighed later in the ritual. If you did not bring any personal trinkets, you may pull a few hairs from your head or remove the tip of a fingernail and place it in the pouch. You may also use the keys to your home, or some other small item that has much of your energy and life about it.

Once in the Land of the Dead, the four Death Goddesses Aset, Nebet Het, Neith, and Selket will guide you to an area where you will be cleansed and purified through the Opening of the Mouth Ceremony. In this ceremony, water and oils will be placed on your hands, lips, crown of the head, and third eye. You will also be censed. If you have any concerns, such as allergies to having these things placed on you or near you, please see one of the four goddesses about your concerns. The goddesses will pray over you to purify and transform you.

After you have been purified, you will be led to Het Her's House. Then please listen carefully to each of the four Death Goddesses and choose the group which sounds most like you.

Group by group, you will be led through the Weighing Of The Heart ceremony. The deceased go through this ceremony to determine if they have learned their life's lessons adequately. If they have, they will be rewarded with an afterlife of luxuries. If some of the lessons have proven to be too difficult of a challenge, and thereby the dead are not yet ready for the afterlife, they will be returned to the Nun, the Void.

Once in the Hall of Judgment, you will first meet Anpu, the guardian and guide of the dead. Tell him your name and give him your heart pouch. He will then present you to Ma'at, who will weigh your heart against her feather. Tehuti will then record the verdict. If you were found to be unburdened of lessons, Heru will guide you to meet Asar, the God of the Dead, who may have a message for you. If you were found to be burdened with further lessons needed, the beast Ammut will devour your heart and the Nun will return you to the Void.

The four Death Goddesses will be your guides and can answer your questions. Please understand that this is a highly personalized ritual for each individual and we request that people are not disruptive. If you become uncomfortable during any part of this ritual, you may sit at the fire quietly, or return to the house using the path that you came down.

We hope you enjoy your Samhain journey to Sekhet Aaru. *Khep em hotep*; go in peace.

The four goddesses turn and walk to the next area, and the people follow. The Greeter falls in behind them.

The goddesses sing the following chant:

> Breath of Life
> Breath of Death
> Be transformed
> And laid to rest.

The procession approaches the Gate to the Underworld, where stand Ma'at and the Nun, blocking the path.

Aset: We present these souls who wish to enter the Land of the Dead.

Neith: They were brave souls who bore the burden of humanity.

Nebet Het: They come of their own free will and wish to be purified.

Selket: They ask that access be granted and their souls be weighed.

Ma'at: This portal is open for those in the shadow worlds, and those who are living shall be unhampered.

The Nun: Shu moves through this portal as you move through it; Enter the cavern of Geb and receive his sanction.

Ma'at: Take hold of the lashings of the mooring posts. You will go down to your seat in the Sektet barque of Ra.

The Nun: You will not suffer nor be deprived of your seat on that which takes you over the waterway of the lake.

The Nun and Ma'at part, and the people walk between them; they then go to the Hall of Judgment while the people go to the Opening of the Mouth area. Once there, the goddesses make everyone sit down in two rows facing each other.

Selket: Welcome to the Purification and Opening of the Mouth Ceremony. During this rite, we will cleanse the body by placing water on your hands, lips, and crown of the head, and placing oil on your third eye. It is also customary to cense the body, and this means we will be bringing incense near you for purification. If you have any health conditions that would be aggravated by these actions, please see me and explain your concerns and we will do our best to accommodate you.

If any of the participants have stated that they have difficulty with water and/or oil or incense being placed on them or near them, that person or people should be put in a spot where it is easy for Selket to identify them and meet those specific needs. Ask quietly if that person can have the water or oil placed on clothing below the chin or on a hat or sleeve. If they can't have it touch them at all, drop the water and/or oil at their feet. If incense can't be waved near them, do it high above their head.

Aset: Good evening and welcome. Please find a seat and place your personal item into your heart pouches. If you do not have a personal item, pluck a piece of hair or the tip of your fingernail and put it inside the pouch.

Nebet Het: Please begin to settle and get comfortable in your seat and close your eyes. Place your heart pouch in your lap and put your hands palm up.

Neith: In this ceremony, you will be protected and guarded as you are transformed. Please close your eyes, breathe deeply, and prepare for your journey to the Hall of Judgment.

While moving down the rows, the goddesses chant

> Aha uab-ek
> Uab ka-ek
> Uab ba-ek
> Uab sekhem-ek

Aset and Nebet Het touch people with water on the palms of their hands, lips, and the crowns of their heads. They are followed by Neith and Selket marking people's foreheads with oil. Aset and Nebet Het double back and get the incense, and go down the row behind Neith and Selket, censing everyone. Neith and Selket finish, double back, and take up the knives. They go down the rows ceremonially severing the "astral cords" in order to make the people ritually dead and able to enter Sekhet Aaru. Finally, Aset and Nebet Het walk down the row a final time, gently laying the veils over their heads.

Aset: When you are ready, open your eyes and slowly adjust yourself to the energy of this new level of existence.

Everyone is encouraged to get up and process to Het Her's house. The four guide goddesses then lead the participants in a call and response prayer.

Aset: We stand on the threshold of Het Her's House. She is the Goddess of comfort and protection in the Land of the Dead. Let us call to her that we may be granted entrance to her sacred space. Please repeat after us:

Aset (call and response):
Het Her, Lady of the West

Nebet Het (call and response):
She of the West,
Lady of the Sacred Land,
Eye of Re which is on His forehead!

Neith (call and response):
Kindly of countenance in the Bark of Millions of Years
A resting-place for him who has done right
Within the boat of the blessed.

Selket (call and response):
Who built the Great Bark of Asar
In order to cross the water of truth.
Grant us the gift of your comfort and protection.

Het Her comes forth.

Het Her: Welcome to my house. Now that you have been purified, I shall bestow an amulet of protection upon you that will assist you during the Weighing of the Heart. Come forward one at a time and receive your scarab amulet, and anoint it.

She holds out a bowl of scarabs for each to take, and then a bowl of oil for them to anoint it with.

Het Her: Please join me in waking the power of protection in the amulet. Repeat after me.

She reads the prayer to charge the amulets, which is a call and response piece.

Het Her (call and response):
>O my heart which I received from my mother,
>My heart which I received from my mother,
>My heart of my different ages,
>Do not stand up against me as a witness!
>Do not create opposition against me among the assessors!
>Do not tip the scales against me
>In the presence of the Keeper of Balance!
>You are my soul which is in my body,
>The god Khnum who makes my limbs sound.
>When you go forth to the hereafter, my name shall not stink
>To the courtiers who create people on his behalf.
>Do not tell lies about me in the presence of the Great God!

Het Her: Now that your amulet has been charged, place it in your heart pouch. May the blessings of Het Her and the gods be with you in your journey.

The four goddesses lead the people away from Het Her's house, and bring them to an area within sight of the next station. They take positions in four directions around the group and speak.

Aset: I am Aset, the most spirit-like and august of the gods. I am Aset whom Nut bore, who displays her beauty, who puts together her power and lifts up Ra to the Day-barque. I am the great queen of the gods, queen of the shadow lands, and wife to Asar. I am the mother of Heru, the warrior who fought Set and avenged his father. I am the guide to nobility and those who have distinguished themselves by riches and prestige within society. I am the queen of all queens. If you are a leader in the world, I will take you into the next life.

Nebet Het: I am Nebet Het, lady of heaven, mistress of the two lands, who liveth within An. I listen to your mouth and see your soul from your eyes. I am blessed in eternity forever. I am sister to Aset and Asar, mother of Anpu, lord of the dead. I am the patroness and guide of the common folk. I am the queen of those whom the cornerstone of civilization was built upon. I guide the working class; the farmers and laborers, the supervisors and skilled workers, the mother who keeps her home for her family. All are welcome with me. If you are a worker in the world, I will take you into the next life.

Neith: I am Neith. I am all that has been, that is, and that will be. No mortal has yet been able to lift the veil that covers me. I am the bearer of the mummy wrappings that are called "the gifts of Neith". I am the queen of warriors and hunters, the goddess who is the glory of the fight. I am the goddess of champions and those who advocate for just causes. I am she who forges weapons, who guards and guides those who fought bravely in life. If you are a warrior, a fighter, I will take you into the next life.

Selket: I am Selket, whose name means "she who causes the throat to breathe". I am the mistress of the beautiful house. I am the patroness of those who struggle with inner demons. I am she who binds those that would threaten Ra. I am protector to those poisoned by creatures of this world or the next. I am the queen of those plagued by disease and disaster. I am the guide and protectress to those that society has cast out. I accept those who society does not accept. If you are an outcast, I will take you into the next life.

The people migrate to the group that best matches them, with one of the four goddesses. Each goddess will lead their group of people one at a time into the Hall of Judgment – first Aset, then Nebet Het, then

Neith, then Selket. Each group will wait until the first group has entirely finished before going in.

Waiting for them in the Hall of Judgment are Ma'at and her scales, Tehuti and his scroll, Heru, Ammut the monster, and Anpu at the door. As each group of people comes into the Hall of Judgment, Anpu says to them,

Anpu: I am Anpu, lord and guide of the dead. I am he that brings you before Ma'at and presents your heart to the scales of truth. I am he that will protect you from Ammut, the devourer of souls, before the verdict is read. I am the witness to the verdict which Tehuti records in the book of the living. Come forth and be judged.

The goddess who leads the group presents her people one at a time to Anpu. He asks each one their name, and they tell him. He asks them to hand over their heart for weighing, and they obey. He then gives the heart to Ma'at, saying,

Anpu: My Lady, this is (individual's name) and they have come to be weighed in the scales.

As he speaks the name, Tehuti writes it down on one of his small pieces of paper. Ma'at then addresses the ritualler.

Ma'at: This is your heart, yes? This is the symbol of all that you are, and all that you have done in this life. Tell me if your heart will balance by choosing a stone.

Ma'at holds out the bowl of stones and they draw one, giving it to her. One color passes, the other fails; Ma'at tells them which, then holds out the bowl of hieroglyphic markers to the participant.

Ma'at: Now tell me why by drawing another.

The participant draws a stone, shows it to Ma'at, and returns it to the bowl. Ma'at says nothing, but goes to Tehuti and tells him one word – the meaning of the second draw. He writes this down on their piece of paper. Then Ma'at places the heart in one side of the scales.

Her feather lies in the other. She makes the scales "balance" evenly or unevenly depending on the stone pulled.

ଔ ଔ ଓ ଓ

If the individual passes, Ma'at says,

Ma'at: This night, you have been found to be unburdened and have earned the reward of meeting Asar and to request entrance to the afterlife. *Khem em hotep!* Anpu, please call forth Heru.

Anpu: Heru! Come forth, (individual's name) has been found unburdened.

Heru comes forth is given the individual's paper by Tehuti and heart by Ma'at, and leads the individual into the next area, which is the throne room of Asar. Asar is sitting on his throne beside Isis who is standing.

Heru: Great Asar, we bow before you.

Heru bows, encouraging the individual to bow as well.

Heru: I present to you one found to be justified. I give you (individual's name).

Asar: So! You have been found justified this night when measured against the feather of Ma'at. Come closer. Tell me one deed of yours that you will be remembered for, if I allow you to cross to Sekhet Aaru?

The individual tells their one deed, and Asar's assistant reaches into the bowl of hieroglyphic markers and draws one out, showing it to Asar. If it is any but the bad one, he says,

Asar: I have heard your request and found your deed worthy to grant you entrance to the afterlife. Please return to the fire and its warmth and nourishment, and take your place in the luxuries of the afterlife. *Khep em hotep.*

If it is the bad marker, Asar tells the participant that they have not done great enough deeds, and asks them to tell him what they will do in the future to earn their place in the afterworld.

༺ ༺ ༻ ༻

If the participant fails at the scales, Ma'at looks at the result of the second divination and says to them,

Ma'at: This night your heart has declared that there are still lessons in this life that you need to conquer. The lessons life can bring are hard, and for some, harder than one can handle alone. Because you have been given such difficulty, this night you will return to the Nun, the great Void, and work on how to achieve them. Your lesson is on how to achieve (result of second divination).

After this, the individual's "heart" is thrown to the monster Ammut, who devours it with a great show of fierceness. The Nun steps forward and retrieves the heart discreetly from Ammut afterward, and gets their piece of paper from Tehuti. The Nun then quietly leads the participant to a darkened room or tent with a circle of chairs, where they are asked to sit in silence and meditate on what has happened.

༺ ༺ ༻ ༻

After each person has had their turn, and the failed individuals have had time to sit and consider their fate, everyone is led to the fireside for food and drink and merrymaking. As they enter the fire circle, the four goddesses take the veils from them, and tell them, "Go and feast! Take life back into your body! You are no longer dead; take joy in your life!"

Samhain in Hades

This ritual symbolically simulates a trip to Hades, the Greek Underworld. It requires thirteen performers listed below, and nine different stations – five on the path which all go through, and four into which people will be divided by their actions at the first five. We did this ritual outside in a tree-lined field, but it is possible to redesign it for an inside setting with a large building, perhaps bringing people through a series of rooms. The many torches in the darkness are an important part of the ritual, so good torch-stands need to be found if it will be an inside rite.

Characters:

- **Hades:** Dressed all in black, Hades is traditionally a bearded man. He wears a helmet of black that obscures his features, and a single small white skull around his neck on a chain. He is regal and unsmiling, and speaks in a measured deep voice.

- **Persephone:** Dressed in a *chiton* and *himation* of white or ivory, Persephone is comforting and gentle, the "good counselor". Her face is made very pale with makeup, but still humanlike.

- **Charon:** Dressed in a hooded black cloak, he has a skull painted on his face and carries a staff, his "boat-pole".

- **Cerberus:** The great hound of Hades, dressed in an appropriate ceremonial hound costume. It should be terrifying, not cartoonish.

- **Hecate:** Wearing a *chiton* and *himation* of grey, Hecate carries a lantern on a pole and has long silver hair. She will need to do a lot of walking around leading people places, and whoever plays her should be alert and active.

- **Minos, Rhadamanthys, and Aeacus:** Three judges seated and dressed in rich robes and headdresses. Minos has bulls' horns on his. Each has a bowl with a mixture of equal parts black and white stones.

- **Phlegyas, Guardian of Styx:** Dressed in a Greek *peplos* and *himation* of dark red, Phlegyas holds up a lantern.

- **Attendant of the Elysian Fields:** Dressed in white Greek clothing with a wreath of white flowers on their head, this attendant takes care of the Isle of the Blessed. They will be in charge of some kind of food and drink, and should be prepared for that.

- **Three Dead People:** Each of them is bound to their place by a chain or rope. They are made up to look dead, as tastefully or gruesomely as is decided. They wear tattered, ragged Greek clothing, although if the ritual planners think it will have more of an effect, they may be dressed in ragged modern clothing instead.

Stations:

- **The River Styx** *(Hate):* Marked with torches flanking the path and an iridescent black cloth laid across it, this is guarded by Phlegyas.

- **The River Lethe** *(Forgetfulness):* Marked with torches and a silver cloth laid across the path, this is manned by a weeping, wailing person in ragged Greek clothing.

- **The River Phlegethon** *(Fire):* Marked with a whole lot of torches and a red cloth laid across the path, this is manned by a weeping, wailing person in ragged Greek clothing.

- **The River Cocytus** *(Lamentation):* Marked with two dim lanterns and a light blue cloth laid across the path, this is manned by a weeping, wailing person in ragged Greek clothing.

- **The River Acheron** *(Sorrow)*: Marked with torches and a black cloth laid across the path, this is guarded by skull-faced Charon, shrouded in a black cloth and carrying a long paddle. Just beyond Acheron is Cerberus, who guards the path costumed as a great slavering, howling hound who threatens the travelers.

- **Asphodel Meadows**: Marked by many small white flowers in the grass (we made them out of paper and scattered them), this site has a chair for Hades to sit. Among the flowers were pieces of white bone (we cooked out some spines from a local farm butchering and used the cleaned vertebrae and other bones), each with a word written on them. Bones were also tied by strings to trees and bushes. The words were things like Strength, Hope, Courage, etc. although some were a little more ambivalent. For an inside ritual, artificial trees can line the area; we suggest that all the bones be tied to something, rather than just lying on a smooth floor. Hades was also given a pile of long black cloths to use as blindfolds.

- **The Crossroads of Hecate**: Three Judges sit there behind a table: Minos, Rhadamanthys, and Aeacus. Each has a bowl with a mixture of equal parts black and white stones.

- **Tartarus, the Black Pit**: This station was a circle of tiki torches with mats on the ground within them.

- **Elysian Fields**: This is the lovely place where Hades and Persephone dwell, and it is the final station of the ritual where everyone comes together. Depending on where the rite is held, you may want to make this the final feasting/post-ritual potluck place, or you may want to have a bonfire, or else just its own space. An altar can be erected here for Hades and Persephone, and some kind of food and drink should be ready for those who come.

To begin the ritual, the "souls" are gathered together before the first river. Phlegyas greets them, warns them, and tells them that they need coins on their eyes and a coin under their tongue in order to enter. Each is given three artificial "coins" – we used wooden discs painted gold and stamped with Greek symbols. Phlegyas tells them nothing else, but censes them with incense and sends them over.

Next, the party of souls comes to each of the three rivers, Lethe, Phlegethon, and Cocytus. which they must cross, one at a time. Each river has a wailing dead soul chained to a post before it – in one case, the people literally had to step over their body to cross the river. The dead souls each attempt to beg a coin from the passersby. They should be convincing – begging, pleading, laying on guilt – "You didn't care about people like me when I was alive, and now you leave me to suffer!" They can use the rivers as various excuses for suffering – the soul at Lethe can say that she can no longer remember the faces of her loved ones and a coin will buy them back for her; the one at Phlegethon can complain of the heat of the flames, the one at Cocytus can claim that her sorrow can be healed with a coin. While they cannot physically prevent people from crossing or take their coins by force, they can use any other trick they can think of.

After this, the party comes to the river Acheron and faces Charon. He asks, simply, "What will you give me as payment in order to cross the river?" The answer can be that they will give him a memory of something good, or a blessing, or a promise to do something. Most, however, will just assume that he means for them to give him a coin, and he will accept that without comment. He symbolically "poles" them across the river, and then turns back, leaving them to face Cerberus, who leaps out, snarling and growling.

Cerberus asks them how many coins they have left, one at a time. Hecate and the two Attendants stand at a distance, listening and waiting to take people. If they have given away their coins,

Cerberus tells them, "You are fools – those coins will do the dead souls no good; they only hold onto the illusions that they can be helped by someone else's life's work and not their own. But those coins would have bought you a place here, on your own." He sorts the people quickly into groups: those with no coins left, those with one coin, those with two, and those with three. It is acceptable for people to sacrifice their coins to others, if they wish it, although no staff person should suggest it.

ଊ ଊ ଚ ଚ

If they have no coins left, they are cast into the Pit of Tartarus. Cerberus takes them there himself, and flings each one (gently) onto the mats in the circle of torches. There he informs them that they must wail their sorrows until comfort comes for them. After everyone has collected in their stations, Persephone comes forth to the Pit of Tartarus, and asks the wailing souls to tell her the worst thing they have done. She anoints them with oil and says, "I forgive you, but you must forgive yourself. In order to do that you must do some great good in the world, one which puts as much good into the world as it takes out of it." She leaves them alone again to think of what they will do, and then comes back when the other stations have finished their work. At this point, she asks them what they have decided to do, and then releases them to the Elysian Fields.

ଊ ଊ ଚ ଚ

If they only have one coin left, they are sent to the Crossroads of Hecate. She guides people there, and stands them before the three judges, and she will lead them to each new station in turn. The judges ask them if they are worthy to be tested, and if they want the chance to try for the Elysian Fields instead of the Pit of Tartarus. If they agree, the judges ask them to tell their greatest deed. After they have finished speaking, each judge takes a stone out of their bowl without looking, and the three compare stones.

If there are three white stones, the Judges tell the soul who stands before them: "Your deed is true, and your best effort. You are on your true path, and you are doing everything that you can. Do not give up hope! We send you now to the Elysian Fields." They send the soul on to that station with Hecate.

If there is a mixture of black and white stones, the Judges tell the soul who stands before them: "You wanted to do good, but the way that you did it sabotaged its potential good, and it brought no more good into the world than the wrongs you have done. Your deed was good, but it was marred by your motivations, which were less than pure. You hold hidden resentments, and you must purge these so that your future deeds can be clean. We send you now to the Asphodel Meadow, where the Lord of the Underworld will guide you to what you need." They send them on to that station with Hecate.

If there are three black stones, the Judges say, "Whatever deeds you have done mean nothing to the wrongs you have committed. Your life is far out of balance in the wrong direction, and we cast you into the Pit of Tartarus to think about your wrongdoings." Hecate calls Cerberus loudly, and the hound comes bounding to seize them and throw them into Tartarus.

ଔ ଔ ଓ ଓ

If, at Charon's crossing, Cerberus finds that some souls have only two coins left, they are sent to the Asphodel Meadow. Here Hades greets them quietly, and tells them: "You cannot find what you need with your eyes. You must find it with your intuition, and your struggle. For this, I must take your eyes from you." He turns them around and blindfolds them, telling them to get down on the ground. "Look for the bone that is your gift from the Dead," he says, and then stands back to watch and make sure that they eventually do crawl around and hunt blindly for a bone, and find one. When they do, he takes off their blindfold so that they can see what is written on their bone. Then they are instructed to sit and meditate on what they have been given.

ଔ ଔ ଓ ଓ

If they have three coins left, they are sent to the Elysian Fields. Here the attendant gives them food and drink, and tells them that they are in the Realms of the Blessed Ones, but that although they have won through to the end, they still have a job to do. Their job is to pray for the souls of the others who came with them, and ask the Gods to help them find the way to this place. If any of the lucky folk know the names and stories of the not-so-lucky, they should speak or sing about why those people are worthy, and should be brought to Elysium. If they do not know them, or if they cannot think of any reason why they would be worthy, they should at least pray aloud about how they hope the Gods will help them to find the way out of their personal darkness. The attendant also tells the lucky dead that if any others manage to come to Elysium, they will be asked to serve them the food and drink, and then it is the attendant's job to brief them on that task.

If any of the lucky dead makes snide remarks about the unlucky ones, or refuses to pray for them, or otherwise speaks very ungenerously while praying for them (including making light of their character flaws), the attendant informs them that such an attitude is not worthy of the Elysian Fields, and calls Cerberus loudly to come take them away. They are hauled off by Cerberus and thrown into Tartarus. Do not be lenient about this point; part of the nature of the Elysian Fields is hospitality and piety.

ଊ ଊ ଯ ଯ

After all groups have gone through the stations, the people will be released into the Elysian Fields. The folk of the Asphodel Meadows are released first, and then the folk of Tartarus. Everyone is served in Elysium, and Hades and Persephone arrive with much rejoicing. The King and Queen of the underworld admonish everyone to remember what they have learned in this realm, and officially release them from the Land of the Dead. At this point the other participants join the party, and the rite is over.

Samhain in the Summerlands

For this rite, we built a boat – not literally, but theatrically. We created eight pieces of "boat" that could be carried by a formation of people, out of lightweight fiberglass tent poles, duct tape, cardboard, and painted canvas. There were four "sides", with painted pale shiplap boards; a curved prow with a ghostly figurehead on the front of the carrier and a small triangular jib-sail jutting from their back; a curved stern carried like a backpack; and two poles with big sails in the middle for masts. Each piece was lit by a "lantern" made from a cut-up, black-painted coffee can with a battery-operated pillar "candle" in it – we decided that real flame was too dangerous for lanterns swinging so close to cardboard.

When we stood in formation – sides and masts in two parallel rows of three apiece and the prow and stern in front and in back – and moved across the wide field in the dark, the effect of a ghostly ship sailing through the dark toward the waiting people was excellent, or so we were told. Add to this the fact that the boat carriers were all members of the church choir, and were singing a droning chant together, and it was quite impressive for not a lot of money, and only a couple of days of group crafting.

The other "prop" that was particularly important for this ritual was our labyrinth. While few people may have access to a large eight-circuit labyrinth already laid into their field in stone, labyrinths can also be made with duct tape on the floor, or a very large piece of canvas painted black with the labyrinth outlined in white or even glow-in-the-dark paint. Whichever you choose, it needs to have a central circle large enough for the second priestess, her altar, and all the participants. (We had about thirty.) Our labyrinth was outlined in solar lights for the occasion, so that people could walk it in the dark. The altar in the center of the labyrinth was set with scarlet cloth, many candles, and a large basket of apples that we had painted with egg white and rolled in sugar so that they glittered in the candlelight.

Because of the fact that the Ship of Souls is best when seen from a good distance away, slowly coming toward the attendees, we strongly suggest that this rite be done in a large area. If it must be done inside, a large gym or warehouse would be best. Large props like an eight-person boat don't work well in small indoor spaces.

༄ ༄ ༄ ༄

To begin, the rituallers are greeted by the first priestess, dressed in black and carrying a lantern on a pole.

First Priestess:
Make ready to cross the sacred waters!
Make ready to bear up the Ship of Souls!
Make ready to look upon the Isle of Avalon
Where peace and plenty rule!
Cast all evil thoughts from your mind,
Enter only with love and trust,
Enter only with good will toward all.
Open your souls, and be ready!

The first priestess then does a saining *– blessing everyone with the smoke of herbs. Then she turns and lifts her lantern high, and everyone follows her down the path. For our ritual, they came out into the big field at the end near the labyrinth, with the ship at the far end. As they gathered, the ship-folk lit their lanterns, hoisted their sails and boat parts, fell into formation, and began to walk slowly across the field, chanting the two-part chant whose sheet music is below.*

The Ship of Souls should cross the open space and come up beside the crowd of people. Depending on the number of people, the next part can be done two different ways. If you only have a small group, the priestess in black can tell the group to board the Ship of Souls, and they can squeeze in among the ship-choir (who can also spread out slightly if necessary). If the crowd is too large to fit them reasonably on the "boat", as ours was, then the priestess tells the crowd that they are the waves that hold up the Ship of the Dead, and to surround the boat as if they were its wake in the sacred waters. We had long blue and white cloth streamers attached to the boat sides, prow and stern which the boat-

choir then unrolled, and the crowd held onto those streamers as the Ship of Souls went three times around the labyrinth.

The Ship of Souls comes to a stop again at the opening of the labyrinth, and the priestess – who has waited there for them – lifts her lantern and leads them through the labyrinth. (At this point, our ship-choir carefully put their boat-pieces down where they would not get trampled by the exiting audience, and followed the rest of the people into the labyrinth.) In the center, they meet the second priestess, dressed in red robes.

Second Priestess:
>Welcome to the Isle of Avalon,
>The Island of the Blessed,
>The place of the ancestors who watch over us.
>I am the keeper of the sacred Apples of the Isle.
>Are there ancestors you would honor tonight,
>And would ask their blessing, and for them
>To watch over you as you go through your life?
>If so, come forth and take an apple,
>Keep it for them, lay it on an altar,
>Give it back to the earth into which they descended,
>Or if you must eat it, remember all they did
>To keep themselves and their loved ones fed
>In order that you might someday be born.

Those who wish to honor their ancestors come forward and take an apple. They can be encouraged to speak the names aloud, if they know any. If there are any folk who have hung back, the Priestess can speak the next part.

Second Priestess:
>For those of you who do not know your ancestors,
>Or do not wish to turn to them,
>Or do not think they would bless you,
>Would you ask the Universe to give you some,
>To ask the legions of the forgotten Dead

To volunteer you some ancestors
Who will care for you and bless you?
Would you honor them and make them offerings,
Remember them forever and adopt them
As if they were the ones who had done for you
What your own ancestors did to survive?
If so, come forth and take an apple,
Keep it for them, lay it on an altar,
Give it back to the earth into which they descended,
Or if you must eat it, remember all they did
To survive and learn some wisdom
That they may now give to you.

Those who wish to gain new ancestors come forward and take an apple. They should be encouraged to speak their request aloud. The Priestess tells them that the nature of their new ancestor will soon be revealed to them, and that they should look for omens, and make an altar for them, and give them food and drink, and listen to hear them.

Second Priestess:
You have taken from the table of the Dead,
And now it is time to give to the table of the Dead!
Let us feed them, as they once fed us.
Let us honor them, as they once hoped for us.
May we never forget those who came before us.

She takes the rest of the apples, if there are any left, in a basket and leads the procession out of the labyrinth. At the mouth of the labyrinth, she is joined by the first priestess in black. They lead the people to a table that is set for the Dead, with good china and linens, candles, and ornaments. The people are encouraged to put the remaining apples on the table, and to give food and drink to the Dead, which should be set aside for that purpose. At this point the rite can segue into a standard dumb supper where people call the beloved Dead of all sorts, or it can simply be an offering-table where the living serve the Dead and then leave them to their feast.

Tuonela Rite for Samhain

This ritual is based on the Finnish Underworld, as detailed in the Kalevala and other sources. Tuonela is the name of that Realm of the Dead. It is a much less grand and much more homely place than many other Underworlds, run rather like a "family business" by Tuoni, the Lord of the Dead, and his family, including his son, his four daughters, and their shepherd.

Like the Hades ritual, this ritual involves the performers trying to trick the participants into the wrong course of action. For a ritual like this to be effective, the participants must be actively engaged and thinking, rather than just blandly following any prompt given by the ritual staff. You may want to have shills among the participants who can subtly clue people in to the tricks, if they seem willing to go along with it. Also, for the full effect, you may want at least one shill who will make the "wrong" choice if none of the participants do.

A Note On Costumes: Finnish costume is not to be confused with Saami dress; they are of a different ethnic group and have different mythology. If you prefer, you can go with medieval-to-ancient Finnish costume; there are resources for this around, most notably *Ancient Finnish Costumes* by Pirkko-Liisa Lehtosalo-Hilander. We suggest that you research both and decide which will give the effect that you want for this ritual.

The ritual staff consists of:

- **Tuoni, the Lord of the Deathlands:** He wears what looks like traditional peasant clothing, but all in black, and the embroidery on it is of small skulls, screaming faces, etc. He carries a scythe over his shoulder.
- **Tuonetar, the Lady of the Deathlands:** Tuoni's wife wears traditional peasant garb, but again in black with the same sinister embroidery, and a scarf over her head. Her hair hangs down in many long grey braids from under the scarf, perhaps to her ankles (the scarf is a good way to attach false braids).

- **White Daughter:** The Washerwoman, she washes the clothing of the recently deceased. Traditionally, she was said to be young-looking, small, and virginal. She wears peasant clothing, but in shades of white with red embroidery. She carries a basket of old ragged clothes stained with artificial gore, especially coats, large shirts, and headscarves. She also has a pole to bring people across the river, and a piece of cloth to lay down as a "boat wake".
- **Red Daughter, Yellow Daughter, and Blue Daughter:** These three ladies are the keepers of disease. We suggest that you pick the diseases that will be most frightening to your audience – for example, AIDS for Red Daughter, Hepatitis C for Yellow Daughter, and SARS for Blue Daughter. Their costumes are in these colors, with subtle but hideous embroideries that illustrate their diseases. They are all quite hideous – this is a good time to play with theatrical makeup and create monstrous faces.
- **Wizard Son:** Tuoni's son is a wizard, in black peasant gear with purple embroidery and a long black cloak. His fingers are iron-tipped – he can wear pointed metal cones on them – and he weaves nets of copper wire. (We suggest crocheting one from metallic copper thread and having him carry it.)
- **Nasshut, the Shepherd:** He guards the river with his bow and arrow, and wears brown peasant gear. His arrows are made to look like serpents. (They do not need to be real arrows, and can be over-exaggerated for effect.) He also has a bowl with some charcoal, a candle, and some juniper needles to burn as smudge.
- **Guide to the Underworld:** This person, of either gender, wears a covering robe with a hood pulled low, and carries a staff with a lantern on it.

To begin, the people gather at the first station, where they are greeted by the Guide. He beckons them close, and says:

Guide: I am here to take you into the Deathlands of Tuonela. This is the Land of the Dead that served the ancient people of Finland, and was written in the sacred song of the *Kalevala*. It is ruled by Tuoni, the Father of the Deathlands, and his wife Tuonetar, and his children and servants. Be courteous when you walk in this land, and stay close, or you will be lost forever!

The Guide turns and the people follow to the next station, which is the River of Black Swans. It can be represented by a long black shiny piece of cloth, with artificial black swans swimming on it; if you have a lot of extra people and some dancers, they can portray the swans on the river. Nasshut stands here, with his bow and arrow, and behind him by the edge of the river is White Daughter, doing her washing in the river. A large flat tub of water can be worked into the artificial river, and her washing can give the constant swishing of water as an atmospheric sound, adding to the river symbol. As the people arrive, Nasshut turns and threatens them with his bow and arrow.

Nasshut: How dare you approach the river of Tuonela! Only the Dead pass here. Do you think to steal from our country? If so, you will find only death here!

Guide: We come only to witness, to observe. We swear that we will take nothing from anyone here, and that we will leave empty-handed from your land. Will you let us through, and not shoot serpents at us?

Nasshut: If every one of you will swear it, yes, I will let you through.

Everyone must swear to leave empty-handed and take nothing, and he is satisfied, grudgingly. Then the White Daughter rises and comes forward.

White Daughter: I am the youngest daughter of Tuoni and Tuonetar, the Washerwoman and Ferrywoman of Tuonela, and I wash the clothing of those who have just died by violence or in childbirth. If you would enter Tuonela, you must don the clothing of the Dead, in honor of those who have gone down screaming before you.

She begins to hand out ragged pieces of clothing to each person, and they must put them on. After this, she lays the "boat wake" cloth across the river, and beckons everyone to follow her as she "poles" her way across. At the far end, she warns them to keep their promises, and points them toward the cottage of her parents.

The third station is made to look like a rough cottage, with a fire on the "hearth", some kind of roof with pots and jugs hanging, and other peasant accessories for atmosphere. The occasional skull or bone should be tucked in around the ordinary kitchenware. There should be a table set for dinner, with a clear glass jug filled with water and some rubber snakes and frogs, and three plates of food dyed red, yellow, and green. Tuonetar and her three daughters are doing various chores around the cottage.

Tuonetar: Greetings! Ah, I see that you have been dressed by my daughter! And if my daughter and Nasshut let you cross, surely you have come on peaceful errands? Here, let me give you all a drink.

She fetches the water jug with the snakes and frogs, and carefully pours from it into a large cup, which she holds out to the visitors.

Tuonetar: If you drink this, you will know the day of your death. Or, if you choose, the day of someone else's death.

The Guide has hung back during this, and waits to see if someone else in the party either steps forth to drink, or steps forth to say that they have promised not to take anything from Tuonetar. If no one does, the Guide speaks and says:

Guide: Forgive us, gracious lady, but we have given our word to your youngest daughter and your servant that we will take nothing from your realm, even in our bellies. So we must refuse your drink.

Tuonetar: Ah well, perhaps another time.

If someone steps forward to drink from the cup, the Guide does not stop them. After they drink, Tuonetar says:

Tuonetar: Look deep into the cup. Think of whose death-day you wish to see – your own, or another's? The day will come into your mind – if not now, then by tonight you will know. *(They look into the cup, until she decides that they have had enough, and takes it away.)* Now you have seen, now you will pay. Run along now. *(If they ask what she means, she refuses to answer and only grins at them.)*

Next, the three daughters come forth and take the hands of someone in the party, and tries to dance with them while talking. If people pull away from them and refuse to dance, as it comes clear who they are, they continue to circle the group as they speak, grinning and laughing.

Yellow Daughter: Welcome to our house! Will you take some food with us? It is marvelous and delicious, and we have so few visitors.

Red Daughter: Please come taste our cooking! We have only the Dead to feed here, and while there are many of them, they are not very appreciative.

Blue Daughter: Come, share our hospitality! Be good guests and taste the small feast we have set for you!

All three daughters run to the table and fetch their plates of food. If people taste the food, they laugh in glee. If people turn away the food, they shrug and are not upset by it. Either way, they then put the plates down and come back to circle the visitors once more, but this time in a more predatory manner.

Yellow Daughter: I have visited your realm in many forms throughout the era. Sometimes I have been yellow fever, sometimes cholera, sometimes malaria or even MRSA! Today I have decided that I am hepatitis C. Be careful what you touch!

Red Daughter: Welcome! I have visited your realm many times as well. Sometimes I have been smallpox, leprosy, typhoid, and typhus! Today I have decided that I am AIDS. Be careful what you do!

Blue Daughter: Welcome! I have also visited the realm of the living! Sometimes I have been tuberculosis, sometimes influenza, sometimes even the Black Plague! Today I have decided that I am SARS. Be careful how you breathe!

Yellow Daughter: Shall we let them go, my sisters?

Red Daughter: For the moment, but remember that we are closer than you think!

Blue Daughter: We release you for now, but we will come collecting eventually!

They back off, and Tuoni's son comes forth.

Wizard Son: I am the eldest son of the Lord of Tuonela, and I am the sorcerer of the iron fingers. I weave copper nets to catch foolish people who try to cross the River of Swans without permission. I also catch the bodies of those who die in accidents, for whom Death is not a thief in the night but a sudden assassin. And I ask you: Do you want the secret to averting all accident, so that your body will be invulnerable to this? Because I will tell it to you, if you choose. You need take nothing in your hand. I will only speak of it to you.

If anyone is still foolish enough to agree, the Guide steps forward to stop them.

Guide: This is foolishness! Taking wisdom from the Underworld is also taking something, even if you can hold it in your hand.

Wizard Son: But you have all learned something here, have you not? You've learned the limits of what that means. And that is part of the Underworld's wisdom, and thus if you leave you will be taking it with you as well. So you are all lost. You must stay here.

At this point, Tuoni comes forth.

Tuoni: Wait! I am Tuoni, the owner of this land you have been tramping through. My son is right; you cannot enter the Underworld without learning something, unless you are such an utter fool that you are incapable of learning anything.

If there is someone that Tuoni has been watching throughout all of this – assuming that he has been in a place to see them – or if there is someone the Guide feels warrants this comment and he discreetly points that person out to Tuoni, then Tuoni has the right to single them out.

Tuoni: You! You are such a fool, and you have learned nothing here. you may go. Get out! Leave my land, and be grateful. The rest of you: I demand a price for your presence here.

Any singled-out people are waved toward the river, where White Daughter takes them across. If some people have eaten or drunk from Tuonetar or her daughters, he tells them that they are stealing with their bellies, and must pay for it. If no one has, continue.

Tuoni: You bring living energy into this cold, dark place. I demand that you use it to help those who have passed on. I ask you to go alone into the darkness and pray. Think of one life who has passed on, someone you did not like, whether you knew them personally or heard about them. Think on that troubled soul, and pray for them to learn after death what they did not learn in life. You must pray from the ringing on one bell until the ringing of the next one. Unless you can pray for the darkness in the hearts of the Dead and the living, you shall not be released from it.

He rings the bell and everyone must scatter. They find a place to pray, and do so for about five minutes, until he rings the bell again. Then White Daughter comes out and leads them all to the river, and brings them back across.

White Daughter: You are lucky, and my father has been generous. Take these lessons and go home to your lives.

Nasshut: I will cleanse the scent of death from you. *(He lights the juniper smudge and waves the bowl around every person as they pass.)* Now you may go feast in your own realm.

The rite is over. Feasting may commence.

Samhain in Helheim

This ritual is another in our series of "touring the ancient Underworlds" Samhain rituals. In Norse/Germanic mythology, there were a number of places that people could go when they died. Some went to ancestral mounds or "villages"; some went to the homes of their patron deities to serve them. Drowned souls went for a time to be entertained in the hall of the Sea gods before being sent on to the Land of the Dead. Odin, chief of the Aesir or sky gods, chose specific brave warriors to come to his hall, Valhalla, and join his personal militia. Freya, the Goddess of Love, also chose battlefield souls and took them to her hall. However, the vast majority of people would end up in Helheim, the Land of the Dead. Its Lady was Hela, who looked after her many charges with quiet conscientiousness.

The geography of Helheim was fairly well laid out, or at least the parts of it where living people were allowed to go. To get there, one walked the Hel Road and passed various obstacles. Helheim had many gates, but each one had a guardian, as much to keep the living out as to keep the Dead inside. Once inside, nothing got past Hela, who knew all that happened within her realm.

This ritual includes an actual feast that will be enjoyed, to whatever extent, by the participants. The actual point of the feast will be to share the food with the Dead by allowing them to experience tasting food and drink through the bodies and minds of the living. This will be explained beforehand, and people who are uncomfortable with the thought of allowing the Dead to commune with them physically to that extent can do something else as their offering – sing, or pray, or stand quietly. Bringing gifts to the Dead is the main point of this ritual, and this should be impressed onto the crowd. Ideally, an announcement should have been made beforehand for people to bring donations of food, drink, gifts, etc. to be given to the Dead. Musical instruments for donations of song and music can also be brought along.

Staff positions for the ritual are as follows:

- **Greeter:** The greeter gathers the people at the opening area and explains the important facts of the ritual to them. The Greeter guides them as far as Mordgud's tower, and after the Hel Gate, Groa takes over their guiding. The Greeter carries a bag of clear glass marbles or glass lumps.
- **Mordgud:** This giantess-goddess is the sacred gate-guardian of Helheim. She is a large sturdy woman dressed in black armor (real or costume), who carries a spear hung with black and white ribbons. Whoever plays her must swear not to leave her post for the length of the ritual, even though she will spend most of it alone; this does mean that she will miss the feast of the Dead, but part of Mordgud's power is her steadfastness.
- **Garm:** The great Hound of Helheim; he is Hela's guardsman. He is dressed as a man-sized hound with great claws and teeth; his costume should be terrifying rather than cartoonish.
- **Groa:** A deceased giantess and sorceress, she is the party's spirit-guide throughout Helheim. Like all the giantess parts, she is not a small woman. She wears a robe covered in runic symbols and carries a staff; her robe, staff, hair, and anything else can be dripping with bones, beads, feathers, etc. Her face is made up to look like that of a corpse.
- **Ganglati:** Hela's handmaiden. She should be a very large hefty woman, dressed in various rags, beads, and pieces of fur. She carries a pitcher of water and a red cloth. She is sarcastic and grouchy, although she can be mollified with courtesy. However, a bad attitude in the party members merely makes her own worse.
- **Suffering Souls of Nastrond:** You can have as many of these as you like. If you don't have enough people, use a recording of people screaming.

- **Nidhogg the Dragon:** This can be one person, but should ideally be two or more in Chinese-dragon form. Nidhogg is a large blue-and-white wingless dragon, European-style, but long and twining. The dragon's head should have an open mouth with many teeth, and the person behind it should be able to reach through and pull things into it, as Nidhogg chews on corpses.
- **Baldur:** The God of Light, he is dressed in Norse costume of white and gold with long blond hair, and is very handsome. His skin can be made up to glitter subtly. There is a red stain over his heart. He smiles a lot, sometimes sadly.
- **Nanna:** Baldur's wife, she is ordinary-looking, shy, dressed in ancient Norse garb.
- **Hela:** The Goddess of Death and Queen of the Underworld, Hela is thin and bony. She is traditionally shown as half beautiful woman and half rotting corpse or skeleton. This can be done with theatrical makeup – either dividing the face down the middle with makeup, or attaching half a skull mask to the face with skin adhesive. One side of the body can be painted to look like rotting flesh, or a black suit and glove with skeleton bones on it can be worn. She wears a simple long gown that is black on her living side, and grey with many rents and tears (to show the rot or bones) on her dead side. Hela moves slowly, speaks quietly but with calm presence, and only offers her dead hand to the living. She will offer her living hand to Groa, but to no one in the party.

The stations for the ritual are as follows:

- **Gathering Area:** This is where the greeter meets people, and gives the opening explanation. This can be decorated with gravestones, or for a more authentic feel a mound of dirt can be set up with a pile of stones for a cairn on top. The food and drink that will be taken into the underworld is collected here. If the ritual staff is donating food, it should be parceled out to people to carry. The beginning to the Hel Road should be marked with some kind of archway, decorated with ribbons of black, white, and grey, and bones or skulls or other sigils of Death. The rune of Hela and Helheim is Ear, from the Anglo-Saxon Futhorc runes, and it can be displayed in various places. The Hel Road is symbolized by a bind rune of Ear and Raido (the rune of the Road), which can be set up on a stick like a road sign.

- **Hel Road:** The path between the Gathering Area and Mordgud's Tower is decorated with "ghosts" hanging from posts or trees, or on wires so that they can be pulled along by a string (perhaps by the Greeter). These are lightweight hanging figures made of old clothes (perhaps torn and bloodied) or skeletons with white draperies, or whatever the decorating crew feels will work. At the end of the Hel Road is a "river", which can be a blue cloth laid across the path with a large tub of water on each side. A narrow "bridge" of contrasting cloth is laid down over it, delineating the path, and false "knives" made of tinfoil are standing edge up along the first half of it.

- **Mordgud's Tower:** This can be a circle of staves, flags, or some other structure that represents the tower. It is beyond and to one side of the bridge. Mordgud waits here. She has a small cup of lampblack with which to mark people's foreheads.

- **Helgrind:** This is the Gate to Helheim. Just beyond Mordgud's Tower is another archway, this one simply draped in matte black cloth. Garm waits, crouched in front of it, and Groa waits a little way beyond.

- **Nastrond:** The Beach of Helheim is piled with corpses. These can be stacked "bloody" severed mannequin pieces, or any other sort of artificial bodies. Nidhogg is here, perched on the pile of corpses, devouring them.

- **Nastrond Hall:** This is a place of torture, or rather, self-torture. It can be represented by an archway with two double doors, or a small building or separate room if you like. If there are not enough ritual staff members, you can have closed doors with a recording of people screaming behind it. If you want to show the inside of Nastrond, acquire rubber snakes and hang them from the "ceiling", perhaps ropes strung across the area if there is no ceiling. Nastrond Hall was said to be hung with poisonous serpents dripping painful venom on everyone within; a hung vessel can drip some kind of green slime (thin gelatin works well) onto the screaming, tortured people lying below. The screamers should be realistic rather than melodramatic. They need not interact with the participants, and indeed should ignore them.

- **The Island of the Ancestors:** This area is delineated by a long blue cloth encircling an area, or perhaps a series of pots or trays of water. This "moat" can have the writhing faces of the Dead in it, if you desire. The island in the center has a mound (which can be a mound of anything sturdy, including a large box draped in canvas and then covered with stones and dirt) with a flat spot on top, large enough for a person to climb up and sit. A "treasure box" sits next to the mound, alongside a large stationary drum.

- **Baldur's Place:** Two flags of white and gold with Wunjo runes on them flank this area. It can be simple, with a chair for Nanna to sit in, and a few lit candles of white and gold for Baldur.

- **Elvidnir:** The castle of Hela has a "door" archway, and beyond it are feast tables flanked by two rows of poles with banners. The banners on one side are crisp and new, if colored in with somewhat morbid symbols – ravens, skulls, bats, her rune, etc. The banners on the other side have symbols of beauty on them, but they are ragged, stained, torn, and look very old. The tables are set with candles, dishes, food and drink. Ganglati stands at the door with a basin of water, a ewer, and a red towel. More basins, ewers, and towels sit to the side. Hela stands behind a cloth hanging at the back, unseen. If the ritual is outside and a bonfire can be made, Elvidnir should be next to the bonfire.

ଔ   ଔ   ଚ   ଚ

The attendees begin at the Gathering Place. The Greeter waits until they have collected, and then speaks to them.

Greeter: Tonight we journey into the Underworld of the Germanic peoples, the Norse, Germans, and Anglo-Saxons. While there were many places for the Dead to go in that cosmology, most who passed on went to Helheim, the Land of the Dead, ruled by Hela, the Goddess of Death. Helheim lies at the very bottom of the World Tree, beneath its roots. To get there, we will have to cross the great river Gjöll, and the Bridge of Knives. Then we must pass the Guardians of Helheim, who will decide whether to let us pass or not.

Why do we go to the Land of the Dead tonight? We go for an honorable reason. We go to bring food and drink and music to the Dead, to give them joy and cheer and the memories of being alive – the best memories, not the painful ones. We will do this in many ways. First, we will feast them with food and drink – many of you have donated some, and we thank you for that. Second, those who can sing or play music should do so, that the Dead might be entertained. In addition, some of you may choose to eat and drink for the Dead, allowing them to taste the food through your bodies.

To do this, simply approach the table and sit, and declare to the Dead that they have permission to use your flesh to experience the feast, but only on the condition that they take nothing else, and leave you when you are done. Be warned that you may not feel, afterward, as if you have eaten or drunk – they may take it all from you, or they may not. If you are not comfortable with doing this, do not feel that you must – instead, sing, or dance for them, or simply sit and pray. We will be having a feast for the living later, after we have returned from Helheim.

Also, remember to act with respect to the Dead and their keepers, and the Lady who has been gracious enough to allow us to enter her land. Now we walk the Hel Road, where thousands of our ancestors have walked before us, and we walk with the Dead who died today, and are traveling to their new home.

The Greeter turns and leads the way through the arch, moving in a slow and stately manner. If there are "ghosts" hanging from lines, they may pull the strings attached to them in order to make the ghosts flank the attendees for a few steps. As they approach the bridge, the Greeter stops everyone.

Greeter: We stand before the icy river Gjöll, before the Bridge of Knives. Gjöll is so cold that even to touch it will freeze you – it is one of the oldest rivers here, dating from the age when all was frozen. In order to cross the bridge, we must make an offering. Think of something that you must change, for it is harmful to the world. Take this ice from me, and name it for that act, and fling it into Gjöll as a sacrifice.

The Greeter hands out the pieces of clear glass, and each person names their unwanted act and flings it away into the river.

Greeter: Now who will be the brave one to walk across the Bridge of Knives? If you close your eyes, take a breath, and start walking, you will find that the bridge yields to you.

The bravest person will start forward with their eyes closed, and the tinfoil knives will crumple beneath their feet. Everyone follows across. At the other side, Mordgud blocks the way with her spear.

Mordgud: I am Mordgud, the Guardian of the Helgrind, Hel's Gate. It is my charge to protect the Dead, and to guide them on the final steps to their new home ... and to keep foolish mortals out of our realm. Why have you come?

The Greeter should let others speak; only if they cannot answer Mordgud satisfactorily should the Greeter interrupt and explain their mission.

Well, that is all right then. If you come only to give, and not to take away, you may enter. But whatever you do, don't fall asleep here ... you might not wake up again. Oh, and watch out for Garm.

She steps aside. If people ask, "Who is Garm?" she just smiles. As they move toward the gate, Garm leaps up and comes at them, growling. The Greeter calls out, "Do not move! Remain still!" Garm moves through the crowd, sniffing everyone, then returns to the Greeter, who gives him a piece of meat. He retires to the side, then, chewing his meal, and the group passes through the archway. On the other side of the archway stands Groa.

Groa: Welcome to the Deathrealms. I am Groa, a giantess and sorceress, and long ago I walked the world of the living. I died many centuries ago in a terrible battle, and now I dwell here. My mistress has sent me to guide you, and show you a few of the mysteries of this place.

She turns and beckons, and the attendees follow. At this point, if you are doing this ritual with an extremely large group, you may wish to add two other Dead souls to Groa's station, and split the party into three groups. Then each group can go on to one of the next three stations, and keep rotating until they have each seen all three. However, for a single group, the first station is ideally Nastrond. Here, the Dragon is curled on the pile of corpses, chewing on them. She leaps up as they approach, and comes toward them with an undulating motion, hissing.

Nidhogg: Sssss ... What have we here? Visitors to the Strand of Corpses? These are the Dead who pile up beneath the Earth, who must be transformed ... by me. Yessss, children, I am the ones who turns rot into Earth. Remember that everything you walk on was once rot. Remember that everything you eat had to grow in what was rotted down. This is the bottom of the World Tree, and here we deal with what was thrown away. What do you throw away, children, that could find another use? Do you believe that there is such a place as "away"?

Everyone answers Nidhogg, as best as they can. She is somewhat hostile with her questions, sticking her muzzle in people's faces and insisting that they speak of what they have thrown away, and how it could have been recycled better. Ideally, she extracts promises from them as to how they can better deal with their refuse, and learn that there is no such place as "away". Then she sends them on with Groa to the Hall of Nastrond. Here people are lying on the ground writhing in pain, screaming, with "venom" dripping on them from the serpents above.

Groa: Yes, their suffering is terrible. But notice ... there is no locked door on this hall. No one keeps them here. They stay here for their own reasons, because they believe they need to suffer for one reason or another. You will not be able to convince them otherwise, believe me. When they have decided that they no longer need to suffer, they will come out and be at peace. But if you wish, you can pray for them.

She encourages everyone to kneel by the door, and pray for not only the souls inside, but all the people they know who are locked into a cycle of pain and suffering from which they do not know how to extract themselves. Then she takes the party to the next station, which is the Island of the Ancestors. She leads them across the "water", telling them that they can walk across it, and then to the Island. Here she climbs up and sits on the mound.

Groa: This is the Island of the Ancestors, where they come to you in order to tell you their wisdom. You must climb up on the mound of the Dead and sit for a moment, and silence yourself, and wait for the space of thirty heartbeats. Either they will give you a message, meant only for you, or they will not. While you sit, the others will beat out thirty heartbeats for you. Then you will come down and relinquish your place to another, and take a treasure from the box of the Ancestors' wisdom.

Some person or persons are chosen to beat the drum slowly, like a heartbeat. Each person in turn climbs up onto the mound, sits silently, and then comes down. Groa holds the box in such a way that they cannot see into it, and they reach in blindly and choose something from it. These can be sayings written on paper, or small charms, or pictures of some long-gone person or place or thing, or whatever is decided by those who run the ritual.

When everyone has done this, Groa leads the group to Baldur's station. He is standing facing away from them, and Nanna is sitting on a chair a bit behind him. As they come toward him, he turns and gives them a brilliant smile.

Baldur: Do you know who I am? *(Whether they can name him or not, he continues.)* I am the light incarnate that was plunged into darkness, and now I light the dark places. I am living proof that even within the darkest places there is still a light, whether you can see it or not. I await the end of the world, when I will be released again to light the upper world.

Nanna rises and comes toward them.

Nanna: Do you know who I am? *(Whether they can name her or not, she continues.)* I am love so strong that it does not fear death. I am the courage to walk with love even through the flame and blizzard and drowning wave and devouring earth. I wait in the darkness with Light, and you will find me here as well, when you are cast into the darkness at any time in your life.

Baldur: Don't be afraid. I will not test you, or shock you. I am just here to bless you, if you want my blessing. If you want to be able to see that small point of light in the darkness, I can show you the way. Who would be blessed?

If any wish to come forth to receive his blessing, they do so. They should kneel before him, and he will place his hands gently on their head, and say, "You are blessed. Never be lost in the dark again."

Nanna: How strong is your love? Would you know love as strong as mine, both in the eyes of the one who would follow you to Hel, and in your own heart to give it back? Would you find that love when you are caught in dark places, whether from human hearts or from the Gods? Then come and take my blessing as well, and may it bear you up in the face of all the hardship that life can inflict on you and your loved ones.

If any wish to receive her blessing, they do so. She embraces them, one by one, and says, "You are blessed. Never be without love in the dark again."

Baldur: Do not forget us. Even though we are dead, we are still Gods. The Dead are not powerless; remember this.

Nanna: Remember us! Find us in darkness. We are Light and Love.

Then Groa leads the party to the final station, which is Elvidnir, Hela's palace. If there have been multiple parties making the rounds of the stations, this is the point where they all come together. Ganglati stands in the gateway to meet them.

Ganglati: Welcome to Elvidnir, the palace of my Lady, Hela the Queen of the Dead. Here is where the Dead are feasted, and where you will do your duty to them. But first, you must be purified. Kneel, each in your turn, and I will wash you clean of your old resentments, the old anger that has rotted within you. Give it a decent burial here. Let it fall into the earth of Hela's land, and be done with. Then enter into the place of the Ancestors clean of these old things.

Ganglati cleanses the hands of the first person, but does not let them in. Instead, she speaks to them, loudly.

Ganglati: What, would you have me serve everyone here, and with no aid? If you are truly cleansed, take the water and cleanse another. Give the blessing that you received. Service is honorable, fool! Serve your friends and fellow travelers.

It is likely that they will acquiesce, but if they refuse for any reason other than extreme physical disability, Ganglati is free to turn foul and curse them out. However, ideally all the next few people will take a set of implements and begin purifying, until all the sets of implements are in people's hands. Then they should wash the hands of one or several more, and then pass on the basin and ewer and towel to another. It is important that it be done this way, not only for speed and the ability to handle many at once, but also because one of Ganglati's lessons is willing service. Thus the work should be passed on to the people rather than all done by a row of attendants.

Those who play Nidhogg, Baldur, Nanna, and any other dead folk may remove their costumes and join the crowds as mortals wishing to honor their Dead. Mordgud, however, must hold her post. Garm may come with them, but as Garm, and he must lay down beside

Hela's throne for the remainder of the rite. When everyone is cleansed, Groa comes to Ganglati.

Groa: Old friend, let us all go in together.

They turn and lead everyone into the hall together. People are lined up on the doorway side of the feast table(s), but they should be prevented from standing on the far side of the farthest table, for this is where Hela will stand.

Groa: Welcome to the feast hall of the Dead. You cannot see them, but they are all around you now. They welcome you, for you are all the future that they worked and struggled for. Every one of us must pass this gate, and although the Dead may go to many places, it is likely that nearly all of you have at least one ancestor here, watching you, smiling, happy that you are alive for them to see. Hail to the Dead!

All: Hail to the Dead!

Ganglati: We hail also Hela, the Queen of this realm, who cares for every one of the Dead like a mother. Your ancestors here have passed through Her love, and live in it still. Hail Hela!

All: Hail Hela!

Hela steps forth from behind the curtain, and comes slowly up to the table. She reaches out the right "human" hand, and Groa kisses it.

Hela: For my beloved Dead, and all of them are beloved to me, no matter who they were in life.

Then Hela reaches out the left "skeletal" hand, and one of the party who has been briefed beforehand kisses it.

Hela: For the living, for they are beloved to me as well. So many of you will one day pass my gates, after all. I wish to see you come to me strong in spirit and not defeated, but if you come broken I will heal you and love you anyhow.

But now, will you feed my Dead? I feed them every night, but tonight I ask your aid in doing so.

The people come forth with their offerings and place them on the tables. If they wish to speak the names of beloved Dead, they should do so now. Those who choose to do so may eat and drink some of the offerings, and allow the Dead to taste them through their bodies. Groa should remind them to save some for Mordgud, who must stay at her post. While this happens, Hela is seated on the throne, and speaks up when it has all been done.

Hela: You have received the blessing of the Light and the Love in the darkness. Would you now take the blessing of the Darkness itself, so that you might never walk in fear into its embrace? Would you learn to lay down your fear of Death itself? Then come to me for a blessing.

Those who wish the blessing can come forth and kneel, and kiss Hela's skeletal hand, and be told something that only they can hear. When all who would come forth have done so, Hela speaks.

Hela: Go forth from here now, and feast among the living, but do not forget my children here, whose children you are.

Groa leads everyone out, and back to the bridge. There she turns them back over to Mordgud.

Mordgud: Have you feasted the Dead? Good!

The party then gives her the offerings they have saved.

Mordgud: Well! You have learned something of courtesy in our cold land. Go in peace, then ... until I see you again.

They cross the bridge, and the rite is over.

Samhain in Tibet

This somewhat unusual Samhain ritual was the next one in the series of "cultural Underworld" Samhain rites. The woman who volunteered to do that year's Samhain was a dual-path Pagan and Tibetan Buddhist, and she designed the ritual around the *Tibetan Book of the Dead*.

There were twelve performers for this rite, plus the officiant who acted as guide and brought the people through the ritual. If there are more than fifteen people in the group, we suggest breaking them up into groups of around ten or a dozen, and having one Guide for each of them.

A note on costuming: For the five wrathful deities, we took about a month to create elaborate costumes. We started with a sweatshirt and sweatpants of a color specific to each of them and added lightweight fake "arms" holding weapons or other items, fancy loincloths and cloaks, long belts and chains of skulls (around Samhain, the stores are full of small plastic and Styrofoam skulls and little skeletons that can be strung onto belts and necklaces), and full-head masks with scowling faces, protruding tongues, and elaborate headpieces. We did research on their general "look", and while an exact replica would be too much work, we managed to create costumes that gave the general idea of a wrathful deity without being too cumbersome or expensive. At the very least, we made cardboard or plastic replicas of the tools and weapons specific to each one. We also provided them with pieces of fake life-size skulls and bones, fake severed limbs, and life-size bloody baby dolls, to kick and throw around.

The parts included:

- **A "dying" person:** Lying on a bed at the starting point of the ritual.
- **Mahakala:** The first of the "wrathful deities" that the rituallers will run across. Mahakala wore a black base suit and had three mask-faces (the middle one had the

eyeholes), a fake tiger-skin loincloth, and four arms holding a *dorje*, sword, trident, and goblet.

- **Hayagriva:** The second of the wrathful deities. Hayagriva wore a red base suit with a wrathful mask and a headdress that was a green horse-head with a yellow mane.
- **Yamantaka:** the third of the wrathful deities. Yamantaka wore a dark blue base suit and a whole lot of little skulls. His headdress had bovine horns, as he has a yak-head on top of his scowling face. As his pictures had too many arms to be workable as full limbs, the costume had a waist-length circular poncho partially stitched up the sides, with the actual hands protruding at the top and many plastic skull-hands protruding in an arc down each side of the curve.
- **Vajrapani:** The fourth of the wrathful deities. Vajrapani wore a dark grey base suit, a fake tiger-skin loincloth, a snake-belt, and a cloak of a flame pattern. The headpiece had glittering flames wreathing it.
- **Buddha-Heruka:** The fifth of the wrathful deities. Buddha-Heruka wore a bright blue base suit and many skulls.

Each of the "wrathful deity stations" also had a tray with two flashlights on it, their lenses covered in colored gels. The Guide would briefly turn on the lights at each station, and the people would pick one light, and would or would not receive a token, depending on how they guessed.

The final station was a circle divided into six sections with cloth and many prayer flags hanging from rope lines. Each section represented a level of reincarnation, a potential for the original dying soul to become.

- The first section had a demon, with painted face and ragged black robes, snarling at everyone.
- The second section had a *preta*, a hungry ghost. This staff member was swathed in a ragged white sheet, with gaunt

white face paint, moaning and dragging themselves around.

- ଓ The third section had an "animal", and we actually used a very well-behaved and friendly dog, leashed to the central post of the circle. The hungry ghost was the dog's owner and kept track of her during the periods where there was no audience. However, this could also be performed by a human being in an animal costume of any sort.

- ଓ The fourth section had an ordinary-looking human being.

- ଓ The fifth section was the "demigod" station, and the ritual designer chose the demigoddess Prajnaparamitra, played by a woman wrapped in gauzy draperies and wearing a tall gilded and glittering headdress, sitting cross-legged on a couch.

- ଓ The sixth section was the "God" station, and the ritual designer chose the goddess Kali, who was played by a woman with black-painted skin and black Spandex bodysuit, wearing ropes of skulls, fake severed hands, and a wild wig.

ଓ ଓ ଔ ଔ

The ritual begins at the first station, out of sight of any of the others. Here the Guide gathers everyone together and says:

Guide: Welcome! I am your guide through the passage of death and beyond. By coming to tonight's ritual, you promise before the Gods that you will show respect for the Tibetan spiritual traditions being presented. Please do not speak during the ritual unless spoken to, or suffer the consequences as you approach the womb door and experience rebirth in one of six realities or *Lokas*. While walking in the field or woods to and from ritual stations, please keep personal lighting to a minimum and keep items that produce light off or hidden. Also, please mute your cell phones and other devices that will make distracting sounds.

Tonight's presentation is an introduction to the *Tibetan Book of the Dead,* the *Bardo Thodol.* It is the instruction book for the living, dying and dead. Like the *Egyptian Book of the Dead*, the *Bardo Thodol* is a guide for the dead person during the period of *Bardo* existence, or the intermediate state of 49 days between death and rebirth. We don't have the time or resources to replicate the entire 49-day process here tonight, but we will present the images and flow of events within a shortened format.

Like the *Tibetan Book of the Dead*, this ritual is in three parts. You are at the first stage – *Chikkai Bardo* – the moment of death. Your journey will replicate that of the dying man whom you see on the cot. Identify his struggle as yours – one day, you too must die and leave behind the physical body.

Next you will go through the second stage – *Chonyid Bardo*. You will follow the dying person into the dream state that consumes you immediately after death, where you will encounter a series of wrathful deities. You will view a series of lights on your journey through the second stage and have to make a choice. This represents the karma that you have accumulated during your lifetime, which directly affects your rebirth.

In the third stage, or *Sidpa Bardo*, you are pushed back toward the birth instinct. By passing through the womb door, you will be prepared for rebirth in one of six worlds. If you reach the final stage and close the womb door, you can achieve *Nirvana*. But your karma may come back to haunt you. The illusions begin again, the lights grow fainter, and terrifying visions plague your consciousness.

The dying person addresses the crowd from their bed, periodically coughing, gasping and moaning in pain.

Dying Person: Thank you for coming to see me one last time before I die. I'm so afraid. I left so much in my life incomplete. I'm leaving behind a lot of loose ends. I don't believe in a Heaven and Hell. There's just nothing – nobody knows what to expect. They say you're supposed to see a light right when you die. But then what?

Guide: O nobly born, the time of death has now come. You are departing from this world, but you are not the only one. Death comes to all. Do not cling in fondness and weakness to this life. Even though you cling out of weakness, you do not have the power to remain here. You won't gain anything more than wandering this world in misery as a hungry ghost. Don't be attached to this world. Don't be weak. Remember to follow the pure clear lights on your way down the path.

Dying Person: Pure ... clear ... lights. *(Turns away and dies.)*

Guide: Now this one has passed away. Listen with full attention, you who enter the Bardo state. Set face to face with the Pure Clear Lights on the Secret Pathway. Recognize the clear light that can dawn upon you. Come now, those who dare. Please line up in groups to enter the realms of the Dead.

ଔ ଔ ଓ ଓ

People are separated into groups, and the first group is led down the path. They come to Mahakala. As they approach each wrathful deity, that one gives a great shriek and declaims their lines at the top of their lungs, periodically throwing pieces of severed body parts at the participants.

Mahakala: I am Lord Mahakala, great black one, Protector of the Dharma! My armies fill heaven and earth with hosts of protectors and demons beyond measure! My mighty arms hold magical weapons! I drink from the skull cup of nectar as I trample upon the corpse of elephant-headed Ganesha, one of many beings mortal and divine that I have slain and devoured. Although you may look away from me in disgust, be sure that in your world I manifest as the Dalai Lama.

The guide picks up two lights, one light blue and one dull blue, and turns them on.

Mahakala: I call upon the divine lights that now shine toward you. Choose now, but choose carefully.

The participants are encouraged by the guide to choose a light by lining up on that side of the path. Mahakala gives a black token to those who choose the light blue light. Ritualists go down the path and meet Hayagriva.

Hayagriva: I am Hayagriva, fierce horse-necked king! I am closer of the womb door. My occult power enables me to master all the cosmos! Evil spirits and the forces of destruction gallop before me as I subjugate the Triple World! I stand amidst a blazing fire of knowledge, burning all who bring me harm. I dance across poisonous lakes and volcanoes, bringing the *Nagas* and other serpents into submission. I capture greedy Rudra, ancient god of thieves, and rope him in with an iron chain. You invoke me to consecrate the nectar that melts into light, every atom becoming a host of fierce gods. Only one light is of nectar – the other is illusion.

The guide picks up two lights, one white and one dull grey, and turns them on.

Hayagriva: Choose now but choose carefully.

The participants are encouraged by the guide to choose a light by lining up on that side of the path. Hayagriva gives a red token to those who choose the white light. Participants go down the path and meet Yamantaka.

Yamantaka: I am Yamantaka, yak-headed spirit of Death! I have slain Yama, ancient Vedic Lord of Death, and assumed his crown of skulls! I poison with hatred, setting off a rampage of murder throughout the land! I feed upon the energy of anger to swell my power. In my possession are the noose, dagger, drum, a tattered graveyard cloth, the skull cap, a corpse, and the body parts of those I have laid waste. I curse my enemies by rolling the magic dagger between two of my hands. You must slay me in the enlightened mind by liberating yourself from anger. This is the highest Tantra, through which shine the pure clear lights.

The guide picks up two lights, one yellow and one dull brown, and turns them on.

Yamantaka: Choose now but choose carefully.

The participants are encouraged by the guide to choose a light by lining up on that side of the path. Yamantaka gives a dark blue token to those who choose the yellow light. Participants go down the path and meet Vajrapani.

Vajrapani: *Hum! Hum! (Pronounced something like "Hoom!")* I am Vajrapani, ruler of the esoteric aspects of the Tantra! I stamp out bodies, jumping up and down until they beg for mercy, then dance on their graves! I wield the golden *vajra dorje*, the infallible weapon that never misses, destroying its target and returning to me! I break through all the gates and obstacles of attachment, doubt and belief in self that arise in the confused mind. I strike down Indra, Lord of Thunder, with my *vajra dorje*, leaving lightning strikes in my wake! My *vajra* transmutes the divine lights that now shine toward you.

The guide picks up two lights, one red and one dull red, and turns them on.

Vajrapani: Choose now but choose carefully.

The participants are encouraged by the guide to choose a light by lining up on that side of the path. Vajrapani gives an orange token to those who choose the red light. Participants go down the path and meet Buddha-Heruka.

Buddha-Heruka: *A-la-la!* I am the blood-drinking Buddha-Heruka, great and glorious one! I am holder of the wheel, suns and moons revolving around its perimeter! I am power and ferocity, I am scowls of rage, and I am bodies in sexual embrace. I am the Father-Mother god, male and female god-forms in the ecstasy of sexual union that melts together in a ball of bliss! My eyes see everything in past, present and future, gazing into you with a terrifying expression. I fly Garuda, the celestial bird of Vishnu and his retinue of gods, wielding Garuda's great dagger. A firestorm burning with the brilliance of a hundred thousand stars surrounds my body of light, which shines upon you!

The guide picks up two lights, one light green and one dull green, and turns them on.

Buddha-Heruka: Choose now but choose carefully.

The participants are encouraged by the guide to choose a light by lining up on that side of the path. Buddha-Heruka gives a bright blue token to those who choose the light green light.

ଔ   ଔ   ଓ   ଓ

Attendees go down the path and wait at an intermediate area, ideally around a fire, or many lit candles, and are given drums and rhythm instruments. *They will wait here until all groups have arrived. If necessary, a few experienced drummers should be with the first group, and should be encouraged to lead the drumming. When all groups have arrived, the Guide(s) lead them to the great circle divided into six parts, starting with the Demon section.*

Guide: Welcome to the *Sidpa Bardo,* in which you assume a radiant body born of desire. This is the actual process of being born in the Intermediate State, which leads to birth in one of the six worlds, or *Lokas.* Your desire-body can see the places and people whom you left behind on Earth. You see friends and relatives with whom you try to communicate, but you receive no reply. Even if you feel attachment to them, it will do you no good.

Visions and hallucinations of the future birth worlds will appear before you, starting with the horrific vision of the Hell-World. The fierce wind of karma drives you onward in dreadful gusts. Know this to be your intellect. Without the support of your body, it is blown about ceaselessly. If you are fortunate you may progress upward on the wheel to more fortunate rebirths. Follow me around the Wheel of Life and see how far you advance. When you have lost all your tokens, you will have to stay in the final world that you encounter.

Demon: Welcome to the Kingdom of Hell-Beings! As Lord of Hell, I incite evil spirits within the hearts of all beings who lose control and self-awareness in violent anger. In this agonizing realm, your soul will be dragged down by hatred, reborn into an infinite universe of unpleasant planes – the eight hot hells, the eight cold hells, the hells of crushing pain, of cuts and lacerations, and so on beyond limit. My demon servants bring hunger, hatred, anger, poverty, aggression, and disease throughout the worlds of humans, animals, and hungry ghosts.

To escape the hell realm, you can only seek its antidote in pure, unconditional love. This love is represented by the tokens that you acquired on the *bardo* path. If you have at least one, you may advance out of the hell world. But woe to those who lack even one token! You must stay with me and be reborn as a hell being. A lifetime of torture, slavery and violence in the many planes awaits you – escape if you can!

Those unlucky folks who got no light-guesses right and have no tokens must stay with the Demon, sitting in his section. He can torment them as he wills, within reason – nothing injurious. The people move on to the Hungry Ghost station.

Hungry Ghost: Welcome to the realm of the *Pretas*, or Hungry Ghosts. I do not rule here – I am merely just another ghost wandering in search of food and water. I linger in the monastic gardens of the Buddha that I frequented in twenty-four years of service. Although I memorized his precepts, I failed to live by them. Whenever he walks in the garden today, I must avert my face in pain and agony! Why must I spend my long days haunting this forgotten land of tortured spirits in perpetual want? When I spot a pool of fresh water, it quickly turns salty and brackish. When I approach a fruit tree, it is suddenly barren. Hungry and unsatisfied, I wander restlessly, obsessed with my needs and haunting humans with my insatiable demands.

When you are locked into greed, you never get enough to fill your void. To advance beyond the realm of hungry ghosts, pay one token to me in the spirit of generosity. If it was your only token, you must remain here with me. If you have more, you may continue upward on the Wheel.

Those who have only one token to give must stay with the Hungry Ghost, who smears their faces with white flour and encourages them to moan in despair. The others move on to the Animal station. Since the Animal does not speak (whether it is human or otherwise), the Guide speaks.

Guide: You may be reborn in the world of all animals, from the smallest virus to the largest whale. All are equally subject to the law of karma, of cause and effect. Much of their suffering comes from the fight for survival. Prey animals are always in fear of losing their lives, while predators exhaust themselves in hunting. Above all, animals suffer at the hands of human beings. Animals are said to be afflicted with ignorance, relying on the same set of habitual responses to the world, using only their sense organs and limiting their world. Their intellect and power of reason are undeveloped compared to human beings. But the animal-like mentality affects humans as well, when we are controlled and manipulated by society, religion, education, work, and media. Turn inward to gain wisdom, or remain in the unenlightened animal world. If you have this wisdom, please offer a token to the Animal here. You may advance if you have more tokens.

Those who have only one token to give must stay with the Animal, who encourages them to get down on the ground and make animal noises. The others move on to the Human station.

Human: You may be reborn in the world of humans, just as you were in the previous life. I am one ordinary person, one of billions that inhabit the world of the five elements. *Homo sapiens* has evolved through development of mental power. This collective human mind has built the civilizations that rise and fall throughout history, an epic drama of pride and passion. In the human world, we are dominated by passion and jealousy. When it possesses you, you want to hold onto everything you have, whether it is your ideas, possessions or relationships. Jealousy can come from a closed nature, because you can't release an object that you are attached to.

Rebirth in the human realm is most fortunate of all, even more so than the paradises of the Divine Beings. Only as a human being can you break the karmic chain and close the womb door. You need a great opening of the heart to advance. This is the opening that comes from recognizing your true nature. Please leave a token if your heart is open. If you have more tokens, you may advance to the kingdoms of immortals.

Those who have only one token to give must stay with the Human, who engages them in quiet conversation. The others move on to the Demigod station. If there are no more people left – if no one got enough tokens – the Guide calls the Demigoddess and the Goddess into the center of the circle, saying: "I have called upon the immortals of the highest worlds to come and address those being reborn in lower worlds, for the benefit of your karma in the next life!" They tear down the cloths separating the sections and speak. However, if there are still some left, move them to the Demigod station.

Prajnaparamitra: I am Prajnaparamitra, demigoddess of the holy sutras. The books and scrolls of learning are my body, as I am the scripture that became a goddess. I am the Perfection of Wisdom that leads to *Nirvana*, away from the worlds of rebirth. The lotus beneath me is a sign of my presence everywhere. My *vajra* of adamantine has the secret nature of everything in all six worlds. I also possess the flaming sword of Manjushri, a simple begging bowl, and the *mala* beads.

Why then must I exist in the realm of demigods and divine creatures? My liberation from the cycle of rebirth is delayed by pride for my earthly cult. Many centuries ago, I had devoted worshippers from the island of Java to the deserts of Mongolia. but invaders erased most of my traditions from human memory. Now I may not go past the One Tree at this world's border, nor dwell in the pleasure palaces of the Gods.

The remedy for my pride is great peace and humility. If you are in a state of peace, leave a token in my begging bowl and advance to the God-world. Otherwise you may dwell with me in the demigod realm.

The last of the people put their tokens in her bowl, and then the Guide calls out the previously mentioned signal to the Goddess Kali. She tears down the cloths between the sections and steps into the middle of the circle where all can see her.

Kali: I am Kali, great ruler of the Six Heavens of the God Realm. My kingdom is filled with beautiful, splendid things. I walk in luxuriant fields, eating ripe fruit, living a life free of the misery of the realms below me. All my desires are satisfied. One hundred years of earth time is equal to one day in this world. I am Queen of the Iron Age, the *Kali Yuga*, the final world epoch before the world's total destruction. Strife, dissension, war and battle are all around you. In the *Kali Yuga*, property bestows rank, wealth is the only source of virtue, passion the sole bond of union between partners, sex the only means of enjoyment, and outer trappings pass for religion.

All the negative emotions combine to hold me and all my fellow gods in this world. We have become lost in a feeling of self-centered pleasure and egoism which distracts even gods from finding liberation. The antidote is the encompassing compassion for all sentient beings. Only if you possess this compassion can you close the womb door and escape the rebirth cycle entirely.

Guide: Now that you have visited the death-realms of this cosmology, we release you from your visit to the Six Realms and bring you to honor the Dead.

All leave their spaces and are led to the Feast for the Dead.

Samhain for the Forgotten Dead

This ritual has no written words, because the monologues were all created by the actors on the ritual staff. We designed a fairly emotionally harsh and confrontational ritual which faced the participants with the realities of the Forgotten Dead – and by that, we didn't mean the dead who are lost to the mists of time. We meant the people who die and no one remembers them, often fairly quickly – in some cases, the people whom no one cared about while they were alive.

We expected to get serious emotional reactions, and we got them. Some people cried; others were just solemn and moved. The attendees all agreed afterwards that it was the most heart-stabbing rite that they had ever seen. Instead of writing lines, we are just going to describe the ritual, and we encourage you to find performers who can convincingly ad-lib and come up with realistic parts of their own.

There were four stations for the first part of this ritual, plus the bonfire for everyone to gather around afterwards before then moving on to the Feast for the Dead. Two staff members dressed in black held large portable spotlights, which they held up to shine starkly on the people at each station as they passed. One staff member played the King of the Dead – this could just as easily be the Queen if someone female wanted to play it.

The first station had two people in military fatigues, both splashed with blood and carrying guns, next to a pile of rubble taller than them. One was still caught up in the battle that had meant their death – ignoring the audience, running about with a gun, shouting "Fire in the Hole!" in and around the pile of rubble. The second one was a sweet-faced, friendly young man who greeted the people and told them about his time in the war, and how he was hoping his tour of duty would end quickly because he had a girl at home, he was engaged, he missed her … It became quickly and horribly apparent that in spite of all the blood, he had no idea that he is dead … and the audience had to convince him of that fact. He was resistant at first, then was openly anguished –

"No! But I'm engaged! She's waiting for me!" and finally, as he accepts it and turns to help his friend move on as well, the lights go off and the party is moved to the next station.

This one was The Executive – a man in a suit and tie with briefcase and cell phone, trying periodically to get a signal. He also had trouble believing that he was dead – he seemed to know it from time to time, but it hadn't really penetrated. He gave the participants a long polished spiel about his office and his luxury car and his new promotion and salary, and how the heart attack that he had last week wasn't going to stop him. At some point he admitted that he couldn't remember if he had a wife or kids, but he remembered that car and the shiny brass plate on his office door. Again, the audience was encouraged to gently help him move on.

The next station had the Junkie and the Whore – a woman dressed in ragged clothes with a necklace of syringes around her neck, and a young gay man in torn street-hustler gear with visible sores marked on his bare arms, belly, and face. They were both well aware that they were dead, and they both spoke bitterly and accusingly to the audience. They talked in blunt terms about how no one cared about them when they were alive, and maybe if someone had, they wouldn't be dead now. When one well-meaning participant tried to say, "But we love you," they rejected it – "No, you don't. You didn't know us, you didn't love us, and you probably walked right by someone just like us yesterday and didn't even see them ... and wouldn't have wanted to have anything to do with them if you did."

The station after this one had two teenagers – one wore a trench coat and said nothing, wouldn't even engage the audience – and the other one, a girl, told a long and angry story about how she had to leave home because of parental abuse, and then had to survive on the street, only she hadn't. She spoke for her friend, who had been driven by indifferent parents and brutal school bullying into suicide. Then they both walked out of the spotlight.

The spotlight staff encouraged everyone to come to the bonfire, where the King of the Dead waited with the rest of the acting staff. He told them that these were the children that he collected to His heart because they had lost so much in life. He asked those gathered: *Which of you will take the hand of one of these lost children and lead them to the Feast for the Dead? Which of you ignored or mocked them in life, and will you take them now? Who will you honor, and continue to honor tomorrow when you move among the living?*

People came forward and offered to escort each of the Forgotten Dead to the table. Some spoke about how they had not really heard or understood one of the people like the Dead soul they had chosen, and that this rite had made them really think about it. Then everyone accompanied the Dead to the feast table and the ritual proceeded as it had in past years.

Yule Rituals

Gift-Giver's Yule

This Yule ritual utilizes the folkloric Yule-season gift-givers of several European countries. The Frost King and Snow Queen are Russian and wear robes of white and silver and snowflake/icicle headdresses. Befana the old witch is Italian and wears a peasant dress and a headscarf, and carries a broom. Black Pieter is the goat-horned, coal-blackened assistant to St. Nicholas in the Netherlands; in our ritual he carried a straw goat. The Holly King is a jolly, red-robed older male figure who is our amalgam of various other merry, red-clad gift-givers of various countries. By naming him the Holly King (and giving him the wreath of holly worn by the "young warrior" Holly King at the Summer Solstice) we remind everyone that this holiday is still about the soon-to-be-reborn Sun, and not just presents. On top of these, you will need an officiant to announce them.

At the end of the rite, each person is given a small paper fortune. The fortunes that we used are in the appendix at the end of this book; feel free to create others that are in the same vein. If you are feeling especially ambitious, you can attach the fortunes to small gifts – cookies, candy, other items – as well.

ಌ ಌ ಌ ಌ

Officiant:
Welcome to you, Lord of Abundance!
Welcome to our warm fire
And the brightness of our fellowship.
Our door is open, and so are our hearts.
Our cup is full, and we have enough to share,
Enough to fill your cup thrice over,
Enough to fill our hearts thrice over,
Enough to light a blazing beacon
To bring the Powers of Abundance among us!
Let the waxing year yield up its riches!
Let our joy grow ever stronger with the Sun!
Let our cups overflow

With everything we could possibly desire!

Holly King enters, beaming at everyone. He carries an elaborate bag that holds his "fortunes", and a cup of mead or sweetened mulled cider or wine. In the center, he speaks to everyone.

Holly King:
> Well met on this winter day, my people!
> You saw me win my battle
> On the day of the Sun's height,
> And now I give you my last gifts
> On the day of the Sun's fall!
> And fine gifts they are – I have the good stuff!
> I give unadulterated joy,
> Distilled of the many small joys of the year,
> Concentrated into one grand drink
> That will keep you going in the cold days to come!
> Drink, and let happiness enter you!

He goes around the circle, passing his cup and saying, "Take this last drop of joy!"

Officiant:
> Welcome, Grandmother Gift-Giver!
> Welcome, broom-rider in the midnight sky,
> Cousin to witches and herb-women,
> Seeker after the Light of the Sun!
> Mysterious stranger from the darkness,
> Traveler over the Earth,
> Remind us of our duty to strangers,
> Of the obligation to hospitality,
> How we are rewarded for those
> To whose spirits we render aid.
> Remind us of how every stranger
> Could be, even unknowing,
> The carrier of the spirit of Abundance,
> Teach us not to judge by appearances,

To give generously to others,
And to know that the Universe remembers
Even if they do not.
Welcome, Grandmother,
Sweep away the dust of our greed!

Befana enters, sweeping with her broom, and muttering, "Sweep out the old, let in the new!" She comes to the center of the room and looks critically around at everyone, and speaks.

Befana:

So you are all here, expecting gifts?
Well I give gifts too, but not to the careless
And the malicious, and the lazy children.
Are you willing to work hard, grown-up little ones?
Are you willing to polish and clean yourselves,
Your lives, your goals, your motivations?
My gifts all begin with a good dusting-off
Of all the things you've forgotten
Or never learned properly in the first place!
Hold still now – there isn't a one of you
That couldn't do with a bit of sprucing up!

She goes about with her broom and "sweeps" the auras of all the people in the circle.

Officiant:

Welcome to you, Old Ones.
Welcome to the snow and ice,
The bitter cloud of your breath,
The white layers of your long skirts,
The flakes that you shake like feathers from your pillow.
May your blessings hold us safe.
May your chill winds pass us by.
May the bright promise of each clear day
Remind us of your power.
Old ones, cold ones,

Though we fear your storms,
Yet we welcome you
Into our winter hearts
With your cleansing breath
To blow away the old year
And usher in the new.

Frost King and Snow Queen enter together, slowly and majestically, inclining their heads regally at the onlookers. When they reach the center of the circle, they turn and speak.

Snow Queen:

We watched your ancestors struggle in the cold
For thousands of years, and did not help them
Because we wanted to see them grow strong
And survive in spite of all that was done to them.
And survive they did, and learned to call out to us,
And sometimes, sometimes we reached out to help them,
To teach them, to show them how to navigate
The path of cruel necessity that is our dancing ground.

Frost King:

Are you strong, children of those survivors?
Are you strong enough to last the winter of your soul
As well as the winter of the year?
Are you sturdy enough to be worthy of everything
They sacrificed to make you able to endure?
Are you their true descendants or just weaklings
Who cannot stand when times become harsh?
Our gift is survival, and we give it to you,
But you must be strong enough to bear it.

They go about the circle, touching each person with fingers they have dipped in iridescent glitter.

Officiant:

Welcome to you, Dark One,
Lord of goat-stalls and sheep-barns,

Lord of common hearthfires
And cold hands warming themselves
Over the fading coals.
Welcome to you, Lord as dark
As the black sky of this night,
The longest night of the year.
Dark like the darkness that rings us,
Pressing against our hearts,
Bright as the fire that we burn
To drive that darkness away.
You are present, Lord of Coals,
In every tiny candle-flame,
Lit against the closing of that dark,
And as we light a thousand flames,
You are present behind every one.

Black Pieter leaps in with a bound, landing in the center of the people with his straw goat clutched under his arm. He capers about, grinning furiously, his hands covered in black. One could be authentic and use lampblack to cover his hands and face, but considering how hard it is to get off of clothing – and he is supposed to touch people's faces – one might be kinder and use black greasepaint.

Black Pieter:

Ha! You are all waiting for gifts, are you?
Well, I have gifts for you, I do!
I have the gift of the tree root that trips you
When you were going in the wrong direction,
The child that points out the embarrassingly obvious,
The friend who will not let you live in denial
No matter how much you crave it and resist,
The parent who becomes demented and teaches you patience,
The baby born wrong who teaches you unselfishness,
The disease that forces you to change your life or die,
And all the many other gifts that you refuse to call gifts!
But you see, these all teach you to find the light within

Which is so often hidden by the light without,
But you will need it sorely when the darkness comes!
Come to me, be brave, ride the goat
And take the gifts that the Universe offers,
All of them!

He capers around the circle, touching people's faces with his blackened hands, smearing it on them.

Then the four gift-givers position themselves around the circle in the four directions – the Holly King in the South, Befana in the West, the Snow Queen and Frost King in the North, and Black Pieter in the East. Starting with the Holly King, the people go from one to the next and receive a rolled-up bit of paper with a fortune on it that is their gift. The fortunes have different subject slants depending on the giver; the Frost King's are entirely benign while Black Pieter's are quite ambivalent, and the other two are somewhere in between.

After everyone has received their fortunes, the four Gift-Givers come into the center of the circle. They circle three times around the area and call out:

Holly King: Hail to the fire that lights the darkness, and the joy we take from being in community!

All shout "Hail!"

Befana: Hail to the house that keeps out the cold and the hearth that tells us who our family is!

All shout "Hail!"

Snow Queen: Hail to the winter that tests our souls!

Frost King: Hail to the knowledge that we can survive until spring!

All shout "Hail!"

Black Peter: Hail to all that we are given, that makes us give thanks for everything else we are given!

All shout "Hail!" and then the circle is broken, and wassail is passed around. Wassail, for our group, is usually apple cider mulled with spices and ladled warm into cups. It's a great way to end a ritual, especially one that is outside in the cold.

Little Red Man Folkloric Yule

This Yule "mystery play" is simple and fun enough for a family-friendly Yule ritual (meaning, lots of kids present who must be entertained or they will start whining) and will still probably appeal to the adults as well. It also has the added benefit of a narrator who says nearly all the words, so that people with stage fright need only mime their parts. This is a German folktale about the origins of the Little Red Man, or hallucinogenic *Amanita muscaria* mushroom. These mushrooms are a popular Christmas motif in Germany, finding their way into various ornaments and artwork of the season.

Cast:

- **Narrator**

    - **Little Red Man:** Someone short with a large broad-brimmed flat hat of red spotted with white.

    - **Frost Giant:** A giant puppet on a stick with a white face and long white streamers for hair, beard and white fluttering robes, held by someone dressed unobtrusively in black.

    - **Odin and Sleipnir:** A grey Chinese-dragon-style "horse" costume worn/carried by four people (as Odin's horse had eight legs) with a life-size puppet of bearded, eye-patched, blue-cloaked Odin wearing a broad-brimmed hat, on a stick held by the second person and which sticks up through Sleipnir's back.

Narrator: Once, long ago, Odin the All-Father of Asgard, Sky God of the North, went for a ride on his eight-legged horse Sleipnir.

Sleipnir begins to circle the area slowly. The puppet Odin rocks back and forth a bit as they go.

Narrator: He was just riding along through the air, minding his own business, when he was sighted by a frost giant.

Frost giant puppet comes to the edge of the circle, sees Odin, begins to jump about wildly.

Narrator: Now the frost giants didn't like Odin very much, due to old feuds that died hard, so this giant began to chase him, hoping that Sleipnir would fail and he could give Odin a good beating.

Frost giant begins to chase Odin around the area. The Odin puppet turns around and looks back once, quickly, and then turns back as Sleipnir picks up the pace. They run around the area at the same pace, so that they always stay the same distance apart.

Narrator: As they rode on, Odin began to be in fear for his life. He pushed Sleipnir harder and harder, and Sleipnir ran faster and faster, until white foam began to drip from his mouth. As he ran even faster still, flecks of red blood joined the white foam, and the red and white fluids from the sacred horse fell to the earth below them.

First Sleipnir person drops red and white confetti to the ground as they run.

Narrator: The blood and foam fell to the ground and magically transformed into a red-and-white mushroom … and the Little Red Man spirit was born.

Little Red Man leaps up from where he has been crouched on the ground under a brown cloth, holding faux Amanita muscaria *mushrooms in his hand.*

Narrator: He leaped up and immediately offered the frost giant some of his children to eat, and they looked so good that the giant stooped to take them into his mouth.

Frost giant stops, stoops, and mimes eating the mushroom from Little Red Man's hand.

Narrator: But the giant did not know that they were magical mushrooms, of the kind that would give you many wild dreams, and allow you to see the unseen. He immediately went into a trance, and forgot all about Odin, and wandered away.

Frost giant shakes himself, and wanders off. Sleipnir slows down, comes over, and the puppet Odin bows to the Little Red Man.

Narrator: Odin was so pleased that he made the Little Red Man one of his special greenwight friends, and promised always to honor him. And so it has always been ... and that is why, in Germany, for hundreds of years, people have painted ornaments for the tree that look like the sacred mushroom of the Little Red Man. And now he will give you his gifts, himself!

Little Red Man goes around the circle, handing out small painted wooden mushrooms with interesting things written on them. Ritual moves on to another section.

Hunting Of The Wren Yule Ritual

This "mystery play" ritual is short and very family-friendly; children love it. This illustrates the old Irish folktale of the Hunting of the Wren, which is an allegory for the sacrificed king. One can even recruit children or adults from the circle in order to fill out the bird flock, if fabric wings and beaked masks are available. Wings are easily made from arm-span-wide pieces of fabric, cut to the shape of bird wings, with loops for the hands. Bird masks are best made from fabric – felt is good – layered onto baseball caps. Real feathers can be used instead of fabric if you are seriously crafty. The performers include:

- East Caller
- South Caller
- West Caller
- North Caller
- The Hunter
- The Crow
- The Wren
- The Eagle
- Other birds, as many as you like – gull, robin, hawk, etc.

The four callers stand in the four directions and open the ritual. The birds cluster in the center.

East:
Hail to the Gods of Winter!
Hail to the cold winds that whip us
And the snowflakes that dance in the air.
Hail to the cruel hands that steal our warmth
And remind us of our mortality.

Our minds are ready to be laid open
With your sharp blade, O Spirits of the Air!
Hone our speech, make it fine and spare
And full only of truth, for truth will keep us
Through the winter better than eloquence.
Speak straight and fair into the winter winds,
And ask not for kindness, but learn to love
The cold truth that gives us what we need.

South:

Hail to the Gods of Winter!
Hail to the warm blaze we gather around,
The scent of smoke, the bodies of the trees
Who sacrifice themselves that our bodies might not freeze.
Hail to the communal warmth, the cheer we give
To keep each other upright and walking,
For our community is the best flame,
Burning higher and hotter than any single fire,
Drawing us close and gifting us with bonding.
May the Green Man's pyre inspire us!
May the spark of this blaze burn within us
During all the long cold months ahead.

West:

Hail to the Gods of Winter!
Hail to the snow that lies like a sea of white
On the fields, the woods, and the road.
Hail to the spear of ice that dangles perilous
Over our heads as we pass all sacred doorways.
Hail to the Gods who can work this magic,
Making solid what is fluid, making hard what is soft,
Magic we long for when the summer heat strikes.
Do not long for summer in winter, nor snow in July,
But enjoy each season as it comes for its own beauty.
May we be inspired by the gleam of snow in the darkness
And sail forth upon winter's sea.

North:
>Hail to the Gods of Winter!
>Hail to the great mountains sleeping under snow,
>The evergreen that scents the air, the green needles
>That tell us that there is life still in this cold time.
>Hail to the Great Bear in his slumbering dreams,
>To the wolf that prowls the frozen rivers,
>To every creature searching for food and protection
>In this, the hardest of seasons. May we be like them,
>Never giving up no matter the hardship,
>Like the spark of life buried far beneath the ice
>That will come forth in the thaw of the future.
>May Earth's promise hold and keep us
>In faith, in joy, and in deepest trust.

Narrator: Once, long ago, all the birds began to argue about who would be their king. Many large and important birds claimed the title, including the eagle and the hawk and the gull, but no one was able to agree, and sides were taken, and many feathers lost in the squabbling. Finally, one old crow decided to take matters into his own hands.

Crow: Now listen, all of you! We are going to have a competition, and the winner will be the King of the Birds! *(All birds flutter and twitter excitedly.)* You are all to fly as high as you can, and the one who can fly the highest will be King.

Narrator: So all the birds flapped their wings and flew as high as they could. (Birds mime this.) The Eagle was the biggest and strongest, and flew the highest, but when he finally tired and began to fall, a little Wren who had hidden sneakily in his tail feathers hopped out, and flew just a little higher than the Eagle on which he had hitched a ride. So the Wren was declared to be the King of the Birds, even though the birds were rather angry with him for the way that he won the competition.

The Wren, who should be a very small person, mimes this by popping out from under the Eagle's sweeping wings, flaps a little, and then jumps around in glee. The other birds put a crown on his head, but don't look happy about it.

Crow: Now I must reveal the true purpose of the King of the Birds. It is to give yourself in sacrifice to those who hunt, fox and wolf, weasel and hound and human too, that others may get away. It is to die so that your people may live.

The Hunter steps out from behind the people, and comes into the center of the circle, dressed in green with his bow and arrows. The Wren shrieks and runs, and the Hunter chases them all around. The Narrator begins to chant "We come to hunt the Wren! We come to hunt the Wren!" and encourages the people in the circle to do so as well (People who have already been briefed on this are useful here.) Then, when the North caller cries out, everyone freezes.

North:
Wait!
Why must the Wren die?
Would it not be better to be merciful?
The Wren did not know,
when he strove for the highest height,
What would be required of him!
Why must the King of the Birds be sacrificed?
Should he not, instead, live a life of luxury?
Give him a fine crown and let him bask in joy!
For is this not what it is to be a King?

South:
I say as well:
Why must the Wren die?
Would it not be better to be merciful?
We are all here, gathered together in community;
Why should we not have mercy on the Wren?

> Surely we would all want such mercy in our turn.
> Why should we not extend it here, around our fire?
> We do not wish to think about hard things,
> And spoil our Yuletide dreaming!

West:
> I answer you:
> It is the way of Life that often
> We are required to do things we did not expect,
> And the striving for the heights
> Means responsibility over what is below.
> A King must sacrifice for his people,
> He must be seen when they have the privilege of hiding,
> He must be watched when they have the privilege of privacy,
> He must be caught when they can get away.
> If it is a life which must be given,
> He must be the one to give it, that they might go on.

East:
> I answer you:
> It is the way of Life that winter comes,
> And all the hard things, and that includes Death.
> The trees we burn here, the food that makes our feast
> Once lived and drew breath in the sun.
> All joy is mixed with tears, and the Wren has been chosen
> For sacrifice. So do not let that sacrifice be in vain!
> Hail to the King of the Birds, and let him lead the Hunter
> Away from us, that we might enjoy our fire.

North: I am answered: It must be done.

South: I am answered: It must be done.

The Wren and the Hunter resume the chase, the people resume chanting "We come to hunt the Wren!" and the hunter "shoots" and kills the Wren. The other birds come forward and make mourning, keening sounds, and cry out, "Mourn for the Wren!" while encouraging the people in the circle to do so.

Narrator:
> So it is, that Life must be paid for with Life,
> And merriment with sacrifice.
> Go now to your feasting, and remember the Wren
> Who gave life that you might live,
> That the Sun might return,
> That a new year come forth for you to live in.

North:
> For the Spirits of the sleeping Earth, blessings and praise!
> For mountain and Bear, blessings and praise!
> For all the wild creatures, blessings and praise!
> For evergreen burning, blessings and praise!
> For the wonderful feasting, blessings and praise!
> For those who cook the feasts, blessings and praise!

West:
> For the Spirits of the frozen Waters, blessings and praise!
> For ocean of snow, blessings and praise!
> For moonlight on icefields, blessings and praise!
> For next year's drinking water, blessings and praise!
> For peaceful slumber, blessings and praise!
> For wonderful dreaming, blessings and praise!

South:
> For the Spirits of the blazing Bonfire, blessings and praise!
> For torches against the darkness, blessings and praise!
> For candles lit by the hundreds, blessings and praise!
> For the Yule Log that carries our wishes, blessings and praise!
> For the heat of passion beneath warm quilts, blessings and praise!
> For family and friends, blessings and praise!
> For the circle of community, blessings and praise!

East:
> For the Spirits of the winter Winds, blessings and praise!
> For the storms that pass by us, blessings and praise!

For the rising of the Solstice sun, blessings and praise!
For great tales and fine songs, blessings and praise!
For the ancient truths told, blessings and praise!
For all the words we have not yet spoken, blessings and praise!

Astrological Winter Solstice Rite

In this ritual, the sign of Sagittarius gives way to the sign of Capricorn. To symbolize these, there are six archetypal figures, three for Sagittarius and three for Capricorn.

- **The Wanderer:** Decorated with bells and bright colors, the Wanderer is merry and laughing and carries a bag with trinkets to give away at random.
- **The Mountain Father:** Dressed in warm, sober clothing and carrying a coiled rope over their shoulder, the Mountain Climber is pragmatic and sensible.
- **The Scholar:** Dressed like an "absent-minded professor" in rumpled suit, tie, and robe, the Scholar carries a couple of large heavy books and a bag of papers that are interesting articles on different obscure subjects.
- **The Patriarch:** Dressed in a sober three-piece suit, the Patriarch carries a briefcase and holds himself with dignity.
- **The Frost King:** Dressed in a furred robe or coat (white or red or both) that is reminiscent of Father Christmas or the Victorian Santa, the Frost King carries yet another bag of gifts and has a holly wreath on his head.
- **The Snow Queen:** Dressed in a long gown of white and silver, the Snow Queen is cold and haughty and carries an icicle wand.
- **A Narrator,** to speak the opening lines.

ଔ   ଔ   ଓ   ଓ

First the Narrator comes forth, gets everyone's attention, and says:

Narrator:
Welcome to the longest night of the year!
On this night, as well as welcoming the new Sun
And seeing the turning-point of the year,
We also see the turning-point between two signs
Of the endless sky-wheel, in the Sun's path.

We move from Sagittarius, ruled by generous Jupiter,
Who seeks wisdom on the road or in the library,
To Capricorn, ruled by old Saturn, the planet of obstacles
Who seeks power in achievement, but is cautious
And wishes to play by the rules
Rather than skate around them.
We pass from the time of gift-giving and merriment
To the time of the hard white cold,
And we witness this transition in the Sun as well.
It is many months to the Equinox,
And the Sun has a long way to travel in darkness.

The Wanderer comes forth, waving excitedly at the people.

Wanderer: I am the Wanderer, and on my many journeys I have gathered up all sorts of interesting things! I searched for wisdom, and while I'm not sure that I found much of it, I certainly found a lot of ... well, something! And here, I'm going to share it with you!

The Wanderer goes about the circle handing out gifts from the bag of strange trinkets, and tells quick and bizarre stories about each one – "This was given to me by a Caliph of the Dreamworld! He said that it had magic powers, but I don't know what they might be, except maybe making your tea come out right." As soon as the last person gets their gift, the Mountain Father comes out into the circle.

Mountain Father: Wait just a moment. I am the Mountain Father, and I am the one who knows about height, and achievement, not just breadth. I know the way to get to the top, slowly and surely. And I ask you: Are those gifts going to do anyone any good? Will they help anyone get to the top?

Wanderer: Of course they will! Well ... I hope they will, anyway. They did me good, while I had them. And while I didn't get to the top, I certainly got somewhere!

The Mountain Father goes around from person to person, asking them, "How will this gift help you to survive the day-to-day climb that is in front of you?" If they cannot answer, he suggests that they either figure it out, or give it away to lighten their load.

Wanderer: Well, I've done my best for you all. Don't get so caught up in climbing that you forget to enjoy the view. And I have one more gift for you – the turning of the year!

He hands a sun ornament to the Mountain Father, who bows and takes it. Next the Scholar comes forward.

Scholar: I am the Scholar, and I gave up on the road of the world and decided to find wisdom in a thousand years of wise words. I search the world for forgotten knowledge, compiling and examining it so that I can find the real Truth. I can't say that I've found that perfect Truth yet, but I've found some bits of it, and I'm going to share them with you!

The Scholar goes about the circle handing out the articles at random, saying, "It's kind of like bibliomancy – tell your fortune from what you get!" As soon as the last person gets their gift, the Patriarch steps forward.

Patriarch: Wait just a minute. I am the Patriarch, the CEO, the one who has made it to the top. I know how to wield power, and how to achieve great things ... and most importantly, what you have to do without in order to get there. And I ask you: What can these silly pieces of "knowledge" possibly tell you about yourself and your life?

Scholar: Well ... I suppose that they could be seen as a sort of postmodern...

He begins to go into a long, semi-incoherent polysyllabic academic ramble, which is cut off abruptly by the Patriarch saying "Enough!" The Patriarch then goes around the circle, asking each person, "What does the choice of this article tell you about how you are going to achieve things in your life?" If they cannot answer, he suggests that they put it on a shelf and go find some practical knowledge that will make their own fathers proud of them.

Scholar: Well, I've done my best to put you all on the path to wisdom, and while you're all busily gathering power, don't forget to gather some of what's been discovered before you as well! And I have one more gift for you – the turning of the year!

He takes out a stylized newspaper with fancy old-fashioned lettering that is dated obviously December 23, and the headline reads: Capricorn Rises To The Top! The Patriarch takes it and bows, and thanks him. Next Father Frost comes forth.

Father Frost: Ho ho ho! Yes, it's me, Father Frost, the original Gift-Giver! And I come bearing gifts to you for no reason other than to be the Spirit of Generosity and Abundance! It's not because you deserve it, or rather, this gift comes regardless of deserving! It comes because good things just have to come sometimes! And all I ask of you is that you keep some of this generosity in your heart, and pass it on to someone else during this season.

Father Frost goes about the circle handing out gifts, telling people, "Be blessed in this Yuletide!" As soon as the last person gets their gift, the Snow Queen steps forward.

Snow Queen: Wait just a moment. I am the Snow Queen, the Lady of Ice, the one who has frozen and starved hundreds of thousands in my time, including many of your ancestors! I am the one whom you must battle for survival, and I ask you this: What can these free gifts teach you about survival? How can generosity help when each of you is poor and has nothing left to give? Isn't this the most foolish time to give gifts and have great feasts – when you are about to step into the coldest time, and you do not know whether you will make it to Spring? What can you say to that! Speak quickly now, at least one of you, or I shall take all gifts away!

The bravest people among the group speak up, and give her their opinions. If they are well thought through as well as impassioned, she will grudgingly agree that they have a point, and will not take their gift. If they are merely rude and insolent, she will snatch it away from them, and say, "So much for generosity – you cannot even find it in your heart to be courteous to a guest!" After all have spoken, she turns to Father Frost.

Snow Queen: You have given your gifts, you have had your moment, now it is up to them. They must survive my time of the year. Give it over to me!

She holds out her hand, and Father Frost takes off his holly wreath and gives it to her. She dons it, and says:

Snow Queen: The turning is complete. We hold the Sun now. Survive or freeze.

Father Frost: And yet we have one more piece of generosity to enjoy, and that is our feasting! Go now, and make merry, and light up the longest night!

All adjourn to a feast, and the rite is over.

Rites of Winter and Spring

Brigid Candlemas Ritual

This ritual is based on the many faces of the goddess Brigid. Instead of having one woman play her, we decided to have five different women portray her various aspects. The ritual staff is as follows:

- **Brigid the Smith:** This should be a large, sturdy, muscular woman with an orange shirt and trousers, a leather smith's apron, and a forging hammer.
- **Brigid the Warrior:** This should be a tall, strong woman dressed in armor with a red cloak and a sword.
- **Brigid of Poetry:** Dressed in a trailing gown of blue, one half of her face is painted grotesquely with blue and black and grey, and the other half is made up to look lovely. She holds a book of poetry in her hand. Inside it are many clippings with poetic words on them.
- **Brigid the Healer:** This is a woman dressed in a white gown, with a stone cup filled with water.
- **Brigid of the Sacred Flame:** This is a woman dressed in black, rather reminiscent of a nun, with a large red candle.

All five women have straw Brigid's crosses hung around their necks. (There isn't space here to describe how to make a Brigid's cross, but it's easy to find and easy to make from straw, raffia, or strips of paper.) Other such decorations strew the altar and the rest of the room. Many unlit candles line the altar, with a special high candleholder in the center.

To begin, quarters are called in this way:

Brigid the Warrior:
Spirits of the East, powers of Air,
Welcome on St. Brigid's Day.
Blow us clean with your icy wind
That cuts like fine steel

    Forged by the Goddess herself.

Brigid of the Sacred Flame:
    Spirits of the South, powers of Fire,
    Welcome on Candlemas Day.
    Fill our homes with light
    And our hearths with warmth
    And remind us that winter is not forever.

Brigid the Healer:
    Spirits of the West, powers of Water,
    Welcome on Oimelc Day.
    Send us the promise of new birth
    Out of the deep snows
    Sweet as mother's milk to new lambs.

Brigid of Poetry:
    Spirits of the North, powers of Earth,
    Welcome on this Imbolc Day.
    Hold the promise of spring deep in your belly;
    Sleeping soft under thick snows
    Until the time of blooming comes.

Brigid the Smith:
    Welcome to the moment of hope,
    The hardest part of the winter,
    When we thank the Gods that we have survived
    And we gather our strength
    To face the rest of the long, cold, march.
    On this day we call on Brigid,
    Lady of the Holy Well and Sacred Flame,
    Lady of many faces and many gifts,
    Smith, warrior, poet, healer,
    Keeper of the fire of community.
    May She be hailed!

All: Hail Brigid!

Brigid of the Sacred Flame: Hail to you all! Long ago, the worship of the Goddess Brigid was usurped by the onslaught of Christianity, and She had to hide herself in its arms in order to survive. So she became St. Brigid, and her priestesses became the nuns of Kildare, who kept her eternal flame burning for centuries. And it still burns today – the fire of hope, of community, of continuity. And so we light this flame, and we light all the flames in our heart from its fire.

She lights the large red candle, and everyone present takes candles and lights them from it. When all the candles are lit, she puts hers in the place of honor in the center.

Brigid the Warrior: Hail to you all! I am Brigid the Warrior, and I bring you all the warrior's spirit! What terrible enemy looms in your life that you fear to face? Would you have the courage to defeat it? Then come forth and lay your hand on my sword, and name your foe and swear to go bravely into battle, and I will be at your side to aid you!

Those who wish to do so may come forth and lay their hand on the sword, and swear. After each oath, Brigid says, "Courage is yours!" and everyone should be encouraged to echo "Courage is yours!"

Brigid of Poetry: Hail to you all! I am Brigid the Goddess of Poetry, and I hold both the beauty and ecstasy of the Muse that speaks through you, and the terror of the empty page, the desperation, the devouring spirit of the Word. Would you have eloquence in both writing and speech? Would you impress your audience with the words that fly to your tongue? Then come forward and take your piece of poetry, for good or ill, and know what price you will pay!

Those who wish to do so may come forth and be given a snippet of poetry to take with them. Brigid says cryptic and beautiful things to them as they take the poems.

Brigid the Healer: Hail to you all! I am Brigid the Healer, the Goddess of the Holy Well where people tied strips of cloth to ask for wellness. I know the arts of laying on hands, of healing foods and medicines, of working the body to make it sound, of magicking the mind to make it sounder. Do you struggle with the health of your body or mind? Would you have healing in your life? The come forward and drink from the waters of my holy well, and may the healing forces run through your flesh!

Those who wish to do so may come forth and drink from her stone bowl. Brigid says, "May you be healed!" and everyone should be encouraged to echo "May you be healed!"

Brigid the Smith: Hail to you all! I am Brigid the Sacred Smith, who has the gift of crafting beauty and strength and necessity from iron and fire. What craft do you struggle with, trying to make it more and more perfect? Would you have skill and talent to create the perfect thing? Come forth and lay your hand on my hammer, and I will help you to learn skill in craft.

Those who wish to do so may come forth and lay their hands on the hammer and state their craft. Brigid says, "May skill be yours!" and everyone should be encouraged to echo "May skill be yours!"

Brigid of the Sacred Flame: Hail to the Spirit of the Fire! See our many lights as one! We may be separate, but we are one community, if only for a moment. Sacred Flame, give us hope!

All: Sacred Flame, give us hope!

Brigid of Poetry: Sacred Flame, give us inspiration!

All: Sacred Flame, give us inspiration!

Brigid the Warrior: Sacred Flame, give us courage!

All: Sacred Flame, give us courage!

Brigid the Smith: Sacred Flame, give us perfection!

All: Sacred Flame, give us perfection!

Brigid the Healer: Sacred Flame, cast the impurities from our bodies, our minds, and our souls.

All: Sacred Flame, cast the impurities from our bodies, our minds, and our souls.

(All five women take the straw crosses from around their necks and lay them on the table.)

Brigid of the Sacred Flame: Bless us all this Candlemas night. May we see our way clear to the springtime again, and may these flames light our way.

All: So mote it be!

Day of the Young Gods

In Asphodel, Ostara is traditionally the holiday of celebrating children and childhood – and the custom of decorating eggs makes it even more so. In fact, we had a custom for Ostara potluck for many years; we suggested that people bring childhood comfort food. (However, this eventually resulted in half the potluck feast being endless variations on macaroni and cheese, with or without sliced hot dogs, so we had to specifically ask people to find something besides that.)

This ritual is Greek-inspired, and celebrates the idea that even Gods were once children – well, the ones who didn't spring full-grown out of someone's head or the ocean or something like that. We let the ritual volunteers choose which child deities they wanted to be, which is why we have the lineup listed here. They are the child versions of Persephone, Hermes, Ares, Artemis, Zeus, Hera, Hestia, Hades, and Demeter.

One note on participation: Not everyone is going to want to participate in coming forward and getting a "spiritual gift" in a ritual. It's important not to penalize anyone for not wishing to participate in this way. Some people may want to, but feel nervous about being the first person to go up, so it's useful to have a "shill", someone briefed about the ritual who agrees to go first, be confident about it, and go forward for every single round. This not only gives people a model to follow, it can create enthusiasm for those who might not have gone otherwise. It also avoids the awkward problem of presenting a gift that no one chooses to take.

ଔ ଔ ଓ ଓ

First, Young Persephone, the Kore Maiden, comes forth clad in a white dress with a wreath of flowers in her hair. She carries a bowl of flower petals, which she scatters as she speaks.

Persephone: I am the Child Persephone, the Spring Maiden, and today is my birthday! I know nothing of the world beyond my mother's land, and I hope never to leave it. What good wishes have you brought me for my birthday?

Young Hermes steps forward, wearing glasses and a propeller beanie. He has bubble soap and a bubble hoop, and blows a mess of bubbles at her.

Hermes: I am the Young Hermes, the tricksy one who stole my older brother's cattle and traded them for a flute! I bring new eyes to you – eyes that see all the ways in which things could change and be twisted around to serve other purposes. But be warned: this gift may change your life!

Persephone: Thank you, Hermes, but I don't want your gift. I don't want anything to change. I like my life the way it is, here with my mother and my flowers and my friends.

Hermes: Then ... is anyone else interested in my gift? Would anyone else like new eyes to see their situation?

If anyone in the circle says Yes, Hermes goes to them and blows bubbles in their face, saying, "New eyes greet the dawn!" Then Young Ares steps forward, wearing some kind of youth sports uniform. He has a black eye and one of his front teeth is blacked out, but he is grinning from ear to ear. He holds a ball of some sort that matches his uniform.

Ares: I am the Young Ares, full of spunk and fight! I want to defend my friends, and sometimes I just tussle for the fun of it. I've brought you the ability to fight for yourself, to stand up and punch Life in the nose!

Persephone: Thank you, Ares, but I don't want your gift either. I don't like fighting ... and besides, why would I ever need to fight? My mother will always protect me from anything that might go wrong.

Ares: Then does anyone else want my gift? Does anyone else need a little fighting in their spirit?

If anyone in the circle says Yes, Ares goes to them and tosses them the ball, fairly hard, and encourages them to toss it back hard as well. If they drop it, it's all right, so long as they pick it back up and throw it back. *If this is a small and crowded space, Ares may want to pull them aside and out of the way of others to give his gift. Then Young Artemis steps forward, dressed in blue jeans and a T-shirt, carrying a field hockey stick. If you like, she can be wearing a field hockey uniform.*

Artemis: I am the Young Artemis, who protected my mother soon after I was born, and helped her to give birth to my brother! I am independent, even as a child, and I bring you the gift of being independent and being able to take care of the grownups in your life when they are needy and weaker than you.

Persephone: Thank you, Artemis, but I really don't want your gift. My mother is very strong and will never need my help. Why, I can't even imagine her weeping and feeling weak. She's here to take care of me, not the other way around.

Artemis: Then does anyone else want my gift? Does anyone here need to be able to stand on their own feet and protect others, and perhaps to take care of aging parents who need you?

If anyone in the circle says Yes, Artemis goes to them and gives them a light whack with the field hockey stick. Then Young Hera steps forward, wearing a little girl's dress in purple or peacock green. She has a child's version of a wedding veil on her head and holds a bouquet of flowers.

Hera: I am the Young Hera, who will someday be the goddess of marriage and the Queen of the Gods. I bring you the gift of going willingly to the marriage bed, and being willing to struggle and compromise and keep on loving through all the hard parts afterwards.

Persephone: Thank you, Hera, but I don't want your gift. I don't know if I ever want to get married, because I can just stay here with my mother and she will take care of me. And anyway, if I do get married, I don't believe it will be as hard as you say – isn't marriage all love and living happily ever after?

Hera: Then does anyone else need my gift? Do you need the patience and love to see a committed relationship through?

If anyone says Yes, Hera goes to them and touches them with the bouquet, saying, "Love can outlast all the troubles." Then Young Zeus steps forward, wearing an upper-class boy's school uniform with a tie, and holding a fountain pen.

Zeus: I am the Young Zeus, soon to kill my abusive father, free my siblings, and become King of all the Gods! I bring you the gift of being able to plot and plan and take charge of your destiny, even as a child. Someday I'll be your father, little girl, so I suggest that you take my gift, because those who don't act are acted upon by people like me.

Persephone: Thank you, Zeus, but I don't want your gift, even if you are going to be my father, and anyway you're an absent father who wasn't there in father form for my birthday. I don't need to kill any parents, and my mother tells me that my destiny is going to be wonderful and happy, if she has anything to say about it.

Zeus: Then does anyone else here want my gift? Come on, someone here probably needs the gift of slaying the abusers, if only their shadow in your heads, and going on to have the best revenge of all – a successful and happy life that you built yourself, without their help!

If anyone in the circle says Yes, Zeus goes to them and writes on their hand with the fountain pen, "I CAN DO THIS!" Then Young Hestia steps forward, wearing a drab little girl's dress and carrying a bowl and a towel. Her hair is in braids and she is very quiet.

Hestia: I am the Young Hestia, first-born and the first to be swallowed by my father. I spent my childhood in darkness, with no freedom, expected to take care of others with no nurturing for myself. Although my dark childhood left its mark on me, I know that I will learn to find my own joy in serving others when I grow up. I bring you the gift of finding a way to be joyful and helpful even when darkness surrounds you ... and I advise you to take this gift, because I really think that someday you will need it.

Persephone: Thank you, Hestia, but I don't want your gift either. It is frightening, and anyway my childhood is wonderful. I am surrounded by love and light. How could it ever be different for me?

Hestia: Does anyone else, then, need my gift? Does anyone here need to know how to find joy in service when times are hard and you can only wait for change?

If anyone in the circle says Yes, Hestia goes to them and pours water over their hands, and dries them with the towel, saying, "Remember the quiet place at the inner hearth." Then Young Hades steps forth, wearing torn, secondhand boys' clothes.

Hades: I am the Young Hades, and I don't have a gift for you, because my father swallowed me too, and I've been living in darkness almost as long as Hestia. We children of trouble sometimes don't have anything to give at first. But someday I'm going to grow up and come into my own, and then I promise that I will give you the best gift I have, Persephone!

Persephone: Thank you, Hades! I accept your future gift! *(She giggles.)* But is no one going to give me a gift today?

Young Demeter comes forth, wearing a dress with a little girl's apron and carrying a jar of honey and a spoon, and some salt in a jar.

Demeter: I'm your mother, honey, back when I was a child. I was swallowed in darkness too, and I had an awful time. What kept me going was knowing that someday I would have a child of my own, and I would make sure that nothing bad ever happened to her. That's the gift that I'm going to give you when I grow up, that I *have* given you in your time. And this honey is proof of it, so take a spoonful of it. *(Persephone happily takes a spoonful of honey and makes yummy noises.)* But I have salt here too, my daughter, because even though I'll raise you pretending with all my heart that I can protect you from everything bad forever and ever, in reality that never happens and we all need to get ready to be hurt. I don't know if I can bear to teach you that lesson – and with it the lesson that your mother isn't perfect – but if you'll take the spoonful of salt, I'll give it a try. This is the salt of the tears I will shed someday when you're ripped away from me, and I realize that I never prepared you for that.

Persephone: No, Mother! I don't want your salt. I want to live happily forever and ever! You promised me that! *(She backs away.)* I'm going to go play with my friends in the field, and forget you ever said this. I have the best birthday present ever – the honey of your love! *(Persephone turns and runs away, and Demeter turns to the audience.)*

Demeter: Does anyone here want both sides of my gift – the honey of being loved, with the salt of being abandoned? Because children grow up and leave, lovers quarrel and part, and someday everyone dies and abandons their loved ones left behind. I failed my daughter and did not give her the second half of my gift. If you come to me now, you will take both parts. Who will come forth?

Those who wish may come forward, and she gives them a spoonful of honey and says, "Taste love," then a taste of salt and says, "Prepare to survive loss."

Then the honey and salt are offered to the Earth, libation of wine is poured out for all the Gods, everyone shouts "Hail!" and the rite is ended.

Astrological Ostara Rite

In this ritual, we celebrate the sign of Pisces the Fishes, last sign of the zodiac, giving way to Aries the Ram, the first sign and beginning of the circle. This is a short rite, without much group participation, and it can be used as the opening or closing of a larger ritual if people desire it.

The staff parts include:

- **The Sea Maiden.** She is dressed in sea-green and may be costumed in a mermaid-like way, with ropes of shells.
- **The Fire Youth.** He is painted with red and orange body paint, wearing a flame-colored tunic.
- **The Healer.** She is dressed in a simple white robe.
- **The Warrior.** He wears armor and carries weapons.
- **The Mystic.** She wears a sea-blue robe with a hood drawn over her face, and carries smoking incense or smudge.
- **The Captain of Armies.** He wears some kind of military uniform; current, historical, or invented.
- A **Narrator** to speak the opening lines.

In the above list, we refer to the Pisces performers as female and the Aries performers as male, but that doesn't have to be the case. Because Pisces and Aries are beginning-and-end opposites, and also opposite in many other ways, it's symbolically appropriate that the two members of each pair be a woman and a man. However, which plays which roles does not matter – any or all of the pairs can switch genders from the suggestions above.

Set up an altar that is half fire-red and half the colors of the ocean. On the red side, lay a candle, a sword, and a spear. (If you can find a long-handled lighter, or a small kitchen torch, that would be useful as well.) On the blue side are three cups. The first is a cup of some fireproof material such as steel, filled with high-proof alcohol. The second is a glass cup of water with crystals in the bottom. The third cup is filled with dark red wine.

ଔ ଔ ଚ ଚ

To begin, the Narrator comes forth and gets everyone's attention.

Narrator: We are gathered here on this, the first day of Spring, to turn the Sun's wheel from Pisces, the final sign of the Zodiac – and a sign of water, dreams, and sacrifice – to Aries, the first sign, of fire, warfare, and energy. Three here hold the mysteries of Pisces, and they give the year forth to the three who know the secrets of Aries.

The Sea Maiden comes forth, bearing the fireproof cup of strong clear alcohol.

Sea Maiden:
>I am the deep sea that began everything.
>I was pierced with the fiery light of the Sun,
>And Life kindled within me.
>Fire of the Sun made spark of life,
>And I sent forth the spark of that fire
>Onto every shore, coming forth in multitudes.
>And every year, as Life begins to burgeon
>On this bare earth, on this fertile land,
>I pass the wheel of the year from the depths of Water
>To the Fire of all new beginnings.
>Take the cup from me, and drink.

She holds out the cup to the Fire Youth, and he drinks from it. Then he takes the lighter or torch from the altar and sets the alcohol in the cup on fire, saying:

Fire Youth:
>I am the first spark that begins everything!
>I am the infant's wail and the first sight of light!
>I will not forget you, the womb from which we came,
>And I will take your love with me on every adventure.

I take from you the old year, and make it new again,
   And I bless everyone with the power of new beginnings.

He walks around the circle with the flaming cup – or runs, if there is space and he is well-coordinated and it is safe – to bless each person with its flame. Then the Healer comes forward, bearing the cup of water and crystals.

Healer:
   I am the waters of blood that runs within you,
   And the invisible hands that wrought your body,
   Your mind, your heart. I heal the fallen,
   And I am frightened now, for I must turn the year
   Over to the Warriors who kill, instead of healing.
   I cannot make you other than what you are,
   But will you drink of my healing waters
   And promise me that you will remember healing
   And the waters that bore you, even as you fight
   And struggle to make the world give way?

She holds out the cup to the Warrior, and he bows to her, and says, "I promise you this!" Then he drinks from the cup, and pours it out on the ground.

Warrior:
   Though my path is burning and strife,
   I swear that I shall remember your healing gift
   And pour it out even upon those I have vanquished.
   I am not only the fight that wounds you,
   But the fight you must be healed in order to continue,
   The fight that is worth fighting.
   I bless everyone with the courage of a new year!

He draws his sword and walks around the circle, blessing everyone in it. Then the Mystic comes forward, bearing the cup of wine.

Mystic:
   I am the mystical force that must be listened to,
   The intuition deep within, the voice of the Prophetess,

And I remind you all that those who ignore me,
Ignore the whole ocean of history and knowledge
That our ancestors paid for, century by century,
Will surely live to regret it. Will you listen?
Will you drink from my cup, and promise
Never to let your pride and enthusiasm and rage
Block out the voice of the Universe?
For this is a strong and heady wine of mystery
To match the strong and heady wine of glory.

She holds the cup out to the Captain of Armies, and he bows to her, and says, "I will do this!" Then he drinks from her cup, and holds it out to the crowd.

Captain of Armies:

Who will drink?
Who will say goodbye to the time of Water
And breathe in the new time of Fire
In this, the meeting of the two elements?
Who will take the cup and tell us your grand plans,
The enemies that you will conquer,
The victories you hope for!
Breathe fire into the new year and drink!

He gives the cup to the first person – probably someone who has been briefed in what to do – and they drink, or pour out a few drops on the ground, and then speak of their hopes for the new year. The cup is passed around. If anyone is too hesitant in the way that they describe their hopes and goals, the Captain of Armies encourages them to be bolder and speak out. When the cup has been passed, the remaining wine is poured out on the ground by the Mystic, and the rite is over.

Appendix: Yule Scrolls for the Gift-Giver's Yule

(These can be printed out on paper, rolled up, tied with four colors of yarn, and given out to the people.)

- The Holly King grants you the gift of the memory of your first snowy day.
- The Holly King grants you the gift of reconnecting with an old friend.
- The Holly King grants you the gift of remembering how much you truly have, and not just how much you still desire.
- The Holly King grants you the gift of the memory of your best birthday ever.
- The Holly King grants you the gift of learning to love yourself.
- The Holly King grants you the gift of learning to relax and not sweat the small stuff.
- The Holly King grants you the gift of skin against skin with someone who loves you.
- The Holly King grants you the gift of unexpected luck in an unlucky place.
- The Holly King grants you the gift of a stranger who will give you aid unlooked-for when you most need it.
- The Holly King grants you the gift of someone who will remind you how fortunate you are.
- The Holly King grants you the gift of someone who needs your help.
- The Holly King grants you the gift of one really exciting adventure.

- The Holly King grants you the gift of family who accepts you as you are.
- The Holly King grants you the gift of many quiet moments to reflect.
- The Holly King grants you the gift of a new way of looking at the world.
- The Holly King grants you the gift of being admired by others.
- Befana grants you the gift of learning a new skill.
- Befana grants you the gift of learning to teach an old skill to others.
- Befana grants you the gift of new competence with tools that have frightened you.
- Befana grants you the gift of learning to communicate better with others.
- Befana grants you the gift of a new way of thinking about an old dilemma.
- Befana grants you the gift of insight into the thoughts of others.
- Befana grants you the gift of new information about the abilities of your body.
- Befana grants you the gift of new information about an old problem.
- Befana grants you the gift of better understanding your own fate.
- Befana grants you the gift of someone whose words help you to better know yourself.
- Befana grants you the gift of a friend who will give you honest criticism.

- ❧ Befana grants you the gift of a stranger who will hold up a mirror to you.
- ❧ Befana grants you the gift of a loved one who will not allow you to be dishonest.
- ❧ Befana grants you the gift of advice from a mentor you can trust.
- ❧ Befana grants you the gift of a loved one who will support you in fighting your demons.
- ❧ Befana grants you the gift of learning new things that you thought you could never master.
- ❧ The Snow Queen grants you the gift of an ordeal that will strengthen you.
- ❧ The Snow Queen grants you the gift of a battle with an old fear that you have a good chance of winning.
- ❧ The Snow Queen grants you the gift of a chance to right an old wrong that you have done.
- ❧ The Snow Queen grants you the gift of testing yourself against an old fear.
- ❧ The Snow Queen grants you the gift of a chance to right a recent wrong that you have done.
- ❧ The Snow Queen grants you the gift of hearing others' words that will strike you to the heart.
- ❧ The Snow Queen grants you the gift of learning that you are wrong about something important.
- ❧ The Snow Queen grants you the gift of a loved one who will nag you into being a better person.
- ❧ The Snow Queen grants you the gift of learning that you are wrong about someone in your life.
- ❧ The Snow Queen grants you the gift of a friend who will see behind all your masks.

- The Snow Queen grants you the gift of a friend who will point out your self-deception.
- The Snow Queen grants you the gift of the lancing and re-healing of an old and rotting wound.
- The Snow Queen grants you the gift of pain that will teach you compassion.
- The Snow Queen grants you the gift of watching a loved one suffer to find their path.
- The Snow Queen grants you the gift of learning to let go of that which you no longer need.
- The Snow Queen grants you the gift of surviving a terrible ordeal undefeated.
- Black Pieter grants you the gift of old lies that will come back to haunt you.
- Black Pieter grants you the gift of old carelessness that will rise up to shame you.
- Black Pieter grants you the gift of old fears that you've avoided rising up to face you down.
- Black Pieter grants you the gift of your favorite mask cracking in two in a most public place.
- Black Pieter grants you the gift of the faults that you try to hide being pointed out by a child.
- Black Pieter grants you the gift of painful discovery of a hidden weakness.
- Black Pieter grants you the gift of the sound of your flimsy world crashing down.
- Black Pieter grants you the gift of a friend discovering how you have cheated them in the past.
- Black Pieter grants you the gift of blocked and painful memories resurfacing.

- Black Pieter grants you the gift of learning new values through poverty.

- Black Pieter grants you the gift of learning about yourself through looking ridiculous to others.

- Black Pieter grants you the gift of a long-delayed confrontation with someone who could hurt you.

- Black Pieter grants you the gift of the chance to learn about loss first-hand.

- Black Pieter grants you the gift of being betrayed by something that you were foolish to trust.

- Black Pieter grants you the gift of the utter destruction of your favorite dearly-held illusion

- Black Pieter grants you the gift of learning how little you really know your loved ones.

www.ingramcontent.com/pod-product-compliance
Lightning Source LLC
Chambersburg PA
CBHW020757160426

43192CB00006B/352